Luther League of New York State

Luther League Hymnal

Luther League of New York State
Luther League Hymnal
ISBN/EAN: 9783337258924

Printed in Europe, USA, Canada, Australia, Japan

Cover: Foto ©Lupo / pixelio.de

More available books at **www.hansebooks.com**

LUTHER LEAGUE HYMNAL

ISSUED BY AUTHORITY OF THE
LUTHER LEAGUE OF NEW YORK STATE

NEW YORK
LUTHER LEAGUE REVIE

Preface

The need of a book especially adapted to young people's meetings is the reason for the existence of this hymnal. It is not intended for the Sunday School, and it cannot take the place of the Church Hymnal. But owing to the rapid development of young people's societies in the Lutheran Church, and the growing interest of their meetings, a special want has been created which this book seeks, in some measure, to meet. The aim of the committee has been to supply in words and music not only that which is fresh and pleasing, but particularly that which is churchly and devotional, and thus to observe the well-known principles of Lutheran hymnology.

Valuable assistance has been given us in our work by Mr. Hubert P. Main, Mr. John R. Beecroft and Mr. Louis van Gilluwe.

We wish also to express our appreciation to those authors who have given us permission to use their hymn-tunes. If any copyrights have been infringed, it has been done unconsciously, and in future editions, if we are informed of the fact, all due acknowledgment will be made.

GEO. D. BOSCHEN,
GEO. C. F. HAAS,
G. U. WENNER,
W. G. THRALL,
GEO. F. MIDDENDORF, Jr.

Reformation Day, 1895.

COPYRIGHT, 1894, BY
BOSCHEN & WEFER CO.
(in trust.)

Opening Service.

A HYMN shall be sung.

A PSALM shall then be read responsively, all standing to the end of the Prayer. At the end of the Psalm shall be sung the

GLORIA PATRI.

Glory be to the Father, and to the Son; And to the Ho-ly Ghost, As it was in the beginning, is now, and ev-er shall be, World with-out end. A - MEN.

PRAYER shall then be offered; the following Collect or any of the Collects on pages ix and x may be used.

Let us pray.

DIRECT us, O Lord, in all our doings, with Thy most gracious favor, and further us with Thy continual help; that in all our works begun, continued, and ended in Thee, we may glorify Thy holy name; and finally, by Thy mercy, obtain everlasting life; through Jesus Christ our Lord. *Amen.*

Then shall the Scripture Lesson be read, and after the lesson another Hymn shall be sung.

TRANSACTION OF BUSINESS.

Closing Service.

A HYMN shall be sung.

One or more Collects (pages ix and x) shall then be said ending with the Collect for Peace here following:

O GOD, from whom all holy desires, all good counsels, and all just works do proceed, give unto Thy servants that peace which the world cannot give; that our hearts may be set to obey Thy commandments, and also that by Thee we, being defended from the fear of our enemies, may pass our time in rest and quietness; through the merits of Jesus Christ our Saviour. *Amen.*

Then all shall unite in the LORD'S PRAYER which may be said or sung as here following.

THE LORD'S PRAYER.

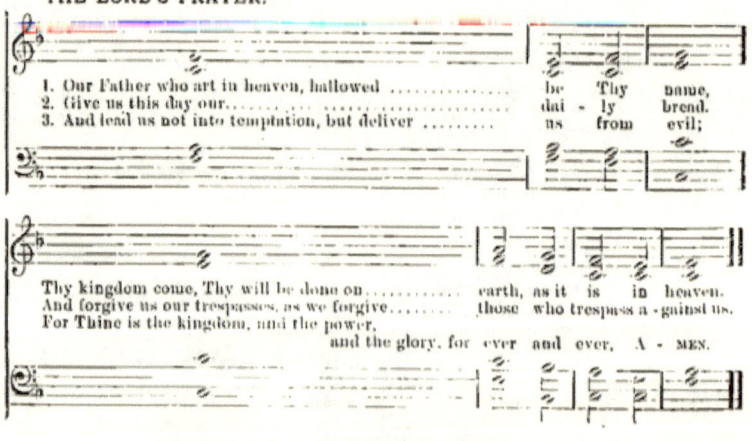

1. Our Father who art in heaven, hallowed .... be Thy name,
2. Give us this day our.......................... dai - ly bread.
3. And lead us not into temptation, but deliver .... us from evil;

Thy kingdom come, Thy will be done on............ earth, as it is in heaven.
And forgive us our trespasses, as we forgive........ those who trespass a - gainst us.
For Thine is the kingdom, and the power, and the glory, for ever and ever, A - MEN.

Psalms.

Psalm 1.

BLESSED is the man that walketh not in the counsel of the ungodly: nor standeth in the way of sinners, nor sitteth in the seat of the scornful.

But his delight is in the law of the LORD: and in His law doth he meditate day and night.

And he shall be like a tree planted by the rivers of water: that bringeth forth his fruit in his season.

His leaf also shall not wither: and whatsover he doeth shall prosper.

The ungodly are not so: but are like the chaff which the wind driveth away.

Therefore the ungodly shall not stand in the judgment: nor sinners in the congregation of the righteous.

For the LORD knoweth the way of the righteous: but the way of the ungodly shall perish.

Psalm 19.

THE heavens declare the glory of God: and the firmament sheweth His handiwork.

Day unto day uttereth speech: and night unto night sheweth knowledge.

There is no speech nor language: where their voice is not heard.

Their line is gone out through all the earth: and their words to the end of the world.

In them hath he set a tabernacle for the sun; which is as a bridegroom coming out of his chamber, and rejoiceth as a strong man to run a race.

His going forth is from the end of the heaven, and His circuit unto the ends of it: and there is nothing hid from the heat thereof.

The law of the LORD is perfect, converting the soul: the testimony of the LORD is sure, making wise the simple.

The statutes of the LORD are right, rejoicing the heart: the commandment of the LORD is pure, enlightening the eyes.

The fear of the LORD is clean, enduring forever: the judgments of the LORD are true and righteous altogether.

More to be desired are they than gold, yea, than much fine gold: sweeter also than honey and the honeycomb.

Moreover by them is thy servant warned: and in keeping of them there is great reward.

Who can understand his errors: cleanse thou me from secret faults.

Keep back thy servant also from presumptuous sins; let them not have dominion over me: then shall I be upright and I shall be innocent from the great transgression.

Let the words of my mouth, and the meditation of my heart, be acceptable in thy sight: O LORD, my strength, and my redeemer.

Psalm 23.

The LORD is my shepherd: I shall not want.

He maketh me to lie down in green pastures: He leadeth me beside the still waters.

He restoreth my soul: He leadeth me in the paths of righteousness for His name's sake.

Yea, though I walk through the valley of the shadow of death I will fear no evil: for thou art with me; thy rod and thy staff they comfort me.

Thou preparest a table before me in the presence of mine enemies : thou anointest my head with oil ; my cup runneth over.

Surely goodness and mercy shall follow me all the days of my life : and I will dwell in the house of the LORD for ever.

Psalm 24.

The earth is the LORD's, and the fullness thereof ; the world and they that dwell therein.

For He hath founded it upon the seas : and established it upon the floods.

Who shall ascend into the hill of the LORD : or who shall stand in His holy place?

He that hath clean hands, and a pure heart; who hath not lifted up his soul unto vanity, nor sworn deceitfully.

He shall receive the blessing from the LORD: and righteousness from the God of his salvation.

This is the generation of them that seek Him; that seek thy face, O Jacob.

Lift up your heads, O ye gates ; and be ye lifted up, ye everlasting doors : and the king of glory shall come in.

Who is this king of glory : the LORD, strong and mighty, the LORD mighty in battle.

Lift up your heads, O ye gates ; even lift them up, ye everlasting doors ; and the king of glory shall come in.

Who is this king of glory : the LORD of hosts, He is the king of glory.

Psalm 46.

GOD is our refuge and strength : a very present help in trouble.

Therefore will not we fear, though the earth be removed : and though the mountains be carried into the midst of the sea.

Though the waters thereof roar and be troubled; though the mountains shake with the swelling thereof.

There is a river, the streams whereof shall make glad the city of God: the holy place of the tabernacles of the Most High.

God is in the midst of her ; she shall not be moved : God shall help her, and that right early.

The heathen raged, the kingdoms were moved: He uttered His voice, the earth melted.

The LORD of hosts is with us : the God of Jacob is our refuge.

Come, behold the works of the LORD : what desolation He hath made in the earth.

He maketh wars to cease unto the end of the earth : He breaketh the bow, and cutteth the spear in sunder ; He burneth the chariot in the fire.

Be still, and know that I am God : I will be exalted among the heathen, I will be exalted in the earth.

The LORD of hosts is with us : the God of Jacob is our refuge.

Psalm 67.

GOD be merciful unto us, and bless us : and cause His face to shine upon us.

That thy way may be known upon earth : thy saving health among all nations.

Let the people praise thee, O God : let all the people praise thee.

O let the nations be glad and sing for joy : for thou shalt judge the people righteously, and govern the nations upon earth.

Let the people praise thee, O God : let all the people praise thee.

Then shall the earth yield her increase ; and God, even our own God, shall bless us.

God shall bless us : and all the ends of the earth shall fear him.

Psalms.

Psalm 72.

GIVE the king thy judgments, O God; and thy righteousness unto the king's son.
He shall judge thy people with righteousness: and thy poor with judgment.
The mountains shall bring peace to the people; and the little hills, by righteousness.
He shall judge the poor of the people, He shall save the children of the needy: and shall break in pieces the oppressor.
They shall fear thee as long as the sun and moon endure: throughout all generations.
He shall come down like rain upon the mown grass; as showers that water the earth.
In His day shall the righteous flourish: and abundance of peace so long as the moon endureth.
He shall have dominion also from sea to sea: and from the rivers unto the ends of the earth.
They that dwell in the wilderness shall bow before Him: and His enemies shall lick the dust.
The kings of Tarshish and of the isles shall bring presents: the kings of Sheba and Seba shall offer gifts.
Yea, all kings shall fall down before Him: all nations shall serve Him.
For He shall deliver the needy when he crieth: the poor also, and him that hath no helper.
He shall spare the poor and needy: and shall save the souls of the needy.
He shall redeem their souls from deceit and violence: and precious shall their blood be in His sight.
And He shall live, and to Him shall be given of the gold of Sheba: prayer also shall be made for Him continually, and daily shall He be praised.
There shall be a handful of corn in the earth upon the top of the mountains: the fruit thereof shall shake like Lebanon; and they of the city shall flourish like grass of the earth.
His name shall endure forever; His name shall be continued as long as the sun: and men shall be blessed in Him; all nations shall call Him blessed.
Blessed be the LORD God, the God of Israel: who only doeth wonderous things.
And blessed be His glorious name for ever: and let the whole earth be filled with His glory. Amen, and Amen.

Psalm 91.

HE that dwelleth in the secret place of the Most High; shall abide under the shadow of the Almighty.
I will say of the LORD, He is my refuge and my fortress: my God; in Him will I trust.
Surely He shall deliver thee from the snare of the fowler: and from the noisome pestilence.
He shall cover thee with His feathers, and under His wings shalt thou trust: His truth shall be thy shield and buckler.
Thou shalt not be afraid for the terror by night: nor for the arrow that flieth by day.
Nor for the pestilence that walketh in darkness: nor for the destruction that wasteth at noonday.
A thousand shall fall at thy side, and ten thousand at thy right hand; but it shall not come nigh thee.
Only with thine eyes shalt thou behold: and see the reward of the wicked.
Because thou hast made the LORD, which is my refuge: even the Most High, thy habitation;

Psalms

There shall no evil befall thee : neither shall any plague come nigh thy dwelling.

For He shall give His angels charge over thee : to keep thee in all thy ways.

They shall bear thee up in their hands : lest thou dash thy foot against a stone.

Thou shalt tread upon the lion and adder : the young lion and the dragon shalt thou trample under feet.

Because He hath set His love upon me, therefore will I deliver Him ; I will set Him on high, because He hath known my name.

He shall call upon me, and I will answer Him : I will be with Him in trouble ; I will deliver Him, and honor Him.

With long life will I satisfy Him ; and show Him my salvation.

Psalm 95.

O COME, let us sing unto the LORD : let us make a joyful noise unto the Rock of our salvation.

Let us come before His presence with thanksgiving : and make a joyful noise unto Him with psalms.

For the LORD is a great God : and a great king above all gods.

In His hand are the deep places of the earth : the strength of the hills is His also.

The sea is His and He made it : and His hands formed the dry land.

O come, let us worship and bow down : let us kneel before the LORD our maker.

For He is our God : and we are the people of His pasture, and the sheep of His hand.

To-day if ye will hear His voice, harden not your heart, as in the provocation : and as in the day of temptation in the wilderness ;

When your fathers tempted me : proved me and saw my work.

Forty years long was I grieved with His generation, and said, It is a people that do err in their heart : and they have not known my ways.

Unto whom I sware in my wrath ; that they should not enter into my rest.

Psalm 100.

MAKE a joyful noise unto the LORD, all ye lands ; serve the LORD with gladness, come before His presence with singing.

Know ye that the LORD He is God : it is He that hath made us, and not we ourselves ; we are His people, and the sheep of His pasture.

Enter into His gates with thanksgiving, and into His courts with praise : be thankful unto Him, and bless His name.

For the LORD is good ; His mercy is everlasting : and His truth endureth to all generations.

Psalm 122.

I WAS glad when they said unto me ; let us go into the house of the LORD.

Our feet shall stand within thy gates : O Jerusalem.

Jerusalem is builded : as a city that is compact together.

Whither the tribes go up, the tribes of the LORD : unto the testimony of Israel, to give thanks unto the name of the LORD.

For there are set thrones of judgment : the thrones of the house of David.

Pray for the peace of Jerusalem : they shall prosper that love thee.

Peace be within thy walls : and prosperity within thy palaces.

For my brethren and companions' sakes ; I will say, peace be within thee.

Because of the house of the LORD, our God ; I will seek thy good.

Collects.

SEND, we beseech thee, Almighty God, thy Holy Spirit into our hearts, that He may rule and direct us according to thy will, comfort us in all our temptations and afflictions, defend us from all error, and lead us into all truth; that we, being steadfast in the faith, may increase in love and in all good works, and in the end obtain everlasting life; through Jesus Christ, thy Son, our Lord. *Amen.*

O LORD God, heavenly Father, who hast given thine only Son to die for our sins, and to rise again for our justification: quicken us, we beseech thee, by thy Holy Spirit, unto newness of life, that through the power of His resurrection, we may dwell with Christ forever; through the same, our Lord Jesus Christ. *Amen.*

FOR THE CHURCH.

GRANT, we beseech thee, Almighty God, unto thy Church, thy Holy Spirit, and the wisdom which cometh down from above, that thy word, as becometh it may not be bound, but have free course and be preached to the joy and edifying of Christ's holy people, that in steadfast faith we may serve thee, and in the confession of thy name abide unto the end; through Jesus Christ our Lord. *Amen.*

FOR THE MINISTERS OF THE WORD.

ALMIGHTY and gracious God, the Father of our Lord Jesus Christ, who has commanded us to pray that thou wouldest send forth laborers into thy harvest: of thine infinite mercy give us true teachers and ministers of thy word, and put thy saving Gospel in their hearts and on their lips, that they may truly fulfil thy command, and preach nothing contrary to thy holy word; that we, being warned, instructed, nurtured, comforted and strengthened by thy heavenly word, may do those things which are well-pleasing to thee, and profitable to us; through Jesus Christ our Lord. *Amen.*

FOR UNITY.

O GOD, who restorest to the right way them that err, who gatherest them that are scattered, and preservest them that are gathered; of thy tender mercy, we beseech thee, pour upon thy christian people the grace of unity, that all schisms being healed, thy flock, united to the true Shepherd of thy Church, may worthily serve thee; through Jesus Christ our Lord. *Amen.*

FOR THE SICK.

ALMIGHTY, everlasting God, the eternal Salvation of them that believe: hear our prayers in behalf of thy servants who are sick, for whom we implore the aid of thy mercy, that being restored to health, they may render thanks to thee in thy Church; through Jesus Christ our Lord. *Amen.*

THANKSGIVING.

ALMIGHTY God, our heavenly Father, whose mercies are new unto us every morning, and who, though we have in no wise deserved thy goodness, dost abundantly provide for all our wants of body and soul; give us, we pray thee, thy Holy Spirit, that we may heartily acknowledge thy merciful goodness toward us, give thanks for all thy benefits, and serve thee in willing obedience; through Jesus Christ thy Son, our Lord. *Amen.*

Collects.

FOR PROTECTION DURING THE NIGHT.

LIGHTEN our darkness, we beseech thee, O Lord; and by thy great mercy defend us from all perils and dangers of this night; for the love of thine only Son, our Saviour, Jesus Christ. *Amen.*

FOR GRACE TO USE OUR GIFTS.

O LORD God Almighty, who dost endue thy servants with divers and singular gifts of the Holy Ghost: leave us not we beseech thee, destitute of thy manifold gifts, nor yet of grace to use them alway to thy honor and glory; through Jesus Christ our Lord. *Amen.*

FOR GRACE TO DO GOD'S WILL.

ALMIGHTY God, give us grace that we may cast away the works of darkness, and put upon us the armour of light, now in the time of this mortal life, in which thy Son Jesus Christ came to visit us in great humility; that in the last day, when he shall come again in his glorious majesty to judge both the quick and the dead, we may rise to the life immortal; through Jesus Christ our Lord. *Amen.*

FOR AID AGAINST TEMPTATION.

O GOD, who justifiest the ungodly, and who desirest not the death of the sinner: we humbly implore thy majesty, that thou wouldest graciously assist, by thy heavenly aid, and evermore shield with thy protection, thy servants who trust in thy mercy, that they may be separated by no temptations from thee, and, without ceasing, may serve thee; through Jesus Christ, thy Son, our Lord. *Amen.*

FOR THE HOLY SPIRIT.

ALMIGHTY and everlasting God, who of thy great mercy in Jesus Christ, thy Son, dost grant us forgiveness of sin, and all things pertaining to life and Godliness: grant us, we beseech thee, thy Holy Spirit, that He may so rule our hearts that we, being ever mindful of thy fatherly mercy, may strive to mortify the flesh, and to overcome the world; and serving thee in holiness and pureness of living, may give thee continual thanks for all thy goodness; through Jesus Christ, thy Son, our Lord. *Amen.*

FOR PURITY.

ALMIGHTY God, unto whom all hearts are open, all desires known, and from whom no secrets are hid: cleanse the thoughts of our hearts by the inspiration of thy Holy Spirit, that we may perfectly love thee, and worthily magnify thy holy name; through Jesus Christ our Lord. *Amen.*

FOR PEACE.

O GOD, who art the author of peace and lover of concord, in knowledge of whom standeth our eternal life, whose service is perfect freedom; defend us, thy humble servants, in all assaults of our enemies; that we, surely trusting in thy defence, may not fear the power of any adversaries, through the might of Jesus Christ our Lord. *Amen.*

FOR AN ANSWER TO PRAYER.

ALMIGHTY God, who hast given us grace at this time with one accord to make our common supplications unto thee; and dost promise that when two or three are gathered together in thy name, thou wilt grant their request: fulfil now, O Lord, the desires and petitions of thy servants, as may be most expedient for them; granting us in this world knowledge of thy truth, and in the world to come life everlasting. *Amen.*

Luther League Hymnal.

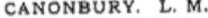

CANONBURY. L. M.   Robert Schumann.

A-wake, my soul, and with the sun Thy dai-ly stage of du-ty run;

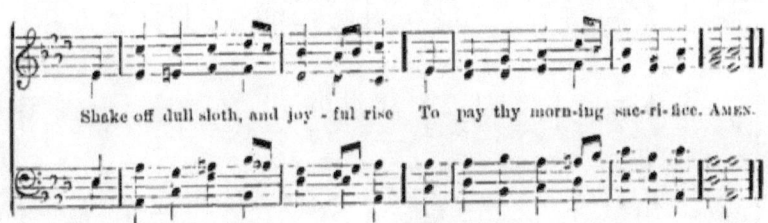

Shake off dull sloth, and joy-ful rise To pay thy morn-ing sac-ri-fice. AMEN.

1

2 Awake, lift up thyself, my heart,
And with the angels bear thy part,
Who all night long unwearied sing
High praises to th' eternal King.

3 Glory to Thee, who safe hast kept,
And hast refreshed me when I slept;
Grant, Lord, when I from death shall wake,
I may of endless life partake.

4 Lord, I my vows to Thee renew;
Scatter my sins as morning dew;
Guard my first springs of thought and will,
And with Thyself my spirit fill.

5 Direct, control, suggest, this day,
All I design, or do or say;
That all my powers, with all their might,
In Thy sole glory may unite.

Thomas Ken.

Morning Worship.

GOTT DES HIMMELS UND DER ERDEN. 8.7.7.
Heinrich Albert.

God who mad-est earth and heav-en, Fa-ther, Son, and Ho-ly Ghost,
Who the day and night hast giv-en, Sun and moon and star-ry host,
Thou whose might-y hand sus-tains Earth and all that she con-tains. A-men.

2 Let the night of my transgression
  With night's darkness pass away:
Jesus, into Thy possession
  I resign myself to-day,
In Thy wounds I find relief
From my greatest sin and grief.

3 Let my life and conversation
  Be directed by Thy Word;
Lord, Thy constant preservation
  To Thy erring child afford.
Nowhere but alone in Thee
From all harm can I be free.

4 Wholly to Thy blest protection
  I commit my heart and mind.
Mighty God! to Thy direction
  Wholly may I be resigned.
Lord, my Shield, my Light divine,
O accept, and own me Thine!

5 Lord, to me Thine angel sending,
  Keep me from the subtle foe;
From his craft and might defending,
  Never let Thy wanderer go,
Till my final rest be come,
And Thine angel bear me home.

Heinrich Albert. Tr. Arthur T. Russell.

Morning Worship

COLUMBIA COLLEGE. 8,4,7.   GEORGE W. WARREN.

Used by permission.

3

2 Pray that He may prosper ever
Each endeavor,
   When thine aim is good and true;
But that He may ever thwart thee,
And convert thee,
   When thou evil wouldst pursue.

3 Think that He thy ways beholdeth;
He unfoldeth;
   Every fault that lurks within;
He the hidden shame glossed over
Can discover,
   And discern each deed of sin.

4 Mayest thou on life's last morrow,
Free from sorrow,
   Pass away in slumber sweet;
And, released from death's dark sadness,
Rise in gladness,
   That far brighter Sun to greet.

5 Only God's free gifts abuse not,
Light refuse not,
   But His Spirit's voice obey;
Thou with Him shalt dwell, beholding
Light enfolding
   All things in unclouded day.

Tr. Henry J. Buckoll.

Morning Worship.

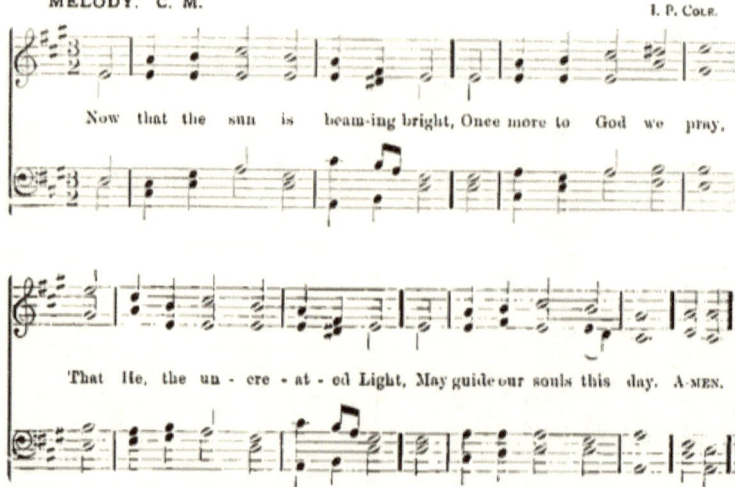

MELODY. C. M.   I. P. COLE.

Now that the sun is beam-ing bright, Once more to God we pray,
That He, the un-cre-at-ed Light, May guide our souls this day. A-MEN.

4
Now that the sun is beaming bright,
  Once more to God we pray,
That He, the uncreated Light,
  May guide our souls this day.

2 No sinful word, no deed or wrong,
  Nor thoughts that idly rove;
But simple truth be on our tongue,
  And in our hearts be love.

3 And while the hours in order flow,
  O Christ, securely fence
Our gates, beleaguered by the foe,
  The gate of every sense.

4 And grant that to Thine honor, Lord,
  Our daily toil may tend;
That we begin it at Thy word,
  And in Thy favor end.
      Tr. John H. Newman.

5
LORD! in the morning Thou shalt hear
  My voice ascending high;
To Thee will I direct my prayer,
  To Thee lift up mine eye:—

2 Up to the hills, where Christ has gone
  To plead for all His saints,
Presenting at His Father's throne,
  Our songs and our complaints.

3 Thou art a God, before whose sight,
  The wicked shall not stand;
Sinners shall ne'er be Thy delight,
  Nor dwell at Thy right hand.

4 Oh, may Thy Spirit guide my feet,
  In ways of righteousness;
Make every path of duty straight,
  And plain before my face.

Evening Worship.

SEYMOUR. 7. *Carl M. Von Weber.*

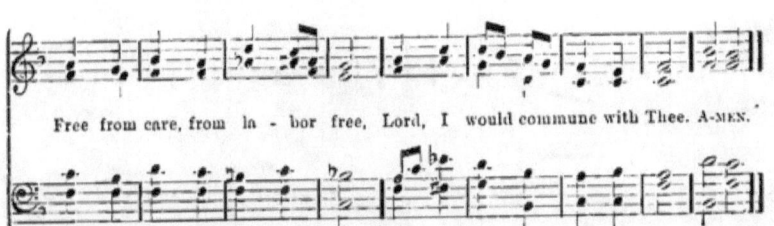

6
Softly now the light of day
Fades upon my sight away;
Free from care, from labor free,
Lord, I would commune with Thee.

2 Thou, whose all-pervading eye
Naught escapes without, within,
Pardon each infirmity,
Open fault, and secret sin.

3 Soon, for me, the light of day
Shall for ever pass away;
Then, from sin and sorrow free,
Take me, Lord, to dwell with Thee.

4 Thou who, sinless, yet hast known
All of man's infirmity;
Then from Thine eternal throne,
Jesus, look with pitying eye.
George W. Doane.

7
For the mercies of the day,
For this rest upon our way,
Thanks to Thee alone be given,
Lord of earth and King of heaven!

2 Cold our services have been,
Mingled every prayer with sin:
But Thou canst and wilt forgive;
By Thy grace alone we live.

3 While this thorny path we tread,
May Thy love our footsteps lead;
When our journey here is past,
May we rest with Thee at last.

4 Let these earthly Sabbaths prove
Foretastes of our joys above;
While their steps Thy children bend
To the rest which knows no end.
O. P., 1826.

Evening Worship.

ST. VINCENT. L. M.

JAMES UGLOW.

Great God, to Thee my eve-ning song With hum-ble

grat-i-tude I raise: Oh, let Thy mer-cy tune my

tongue, And fill my heart with live-ly praise. A-MEN.

2 My days unclouded as they pass,
  And every onward rolling hour,
Are monuments of wondrous grace,
  And witness to Thy love and power.

3 And yet this thoughtless, wretched heart,
  Too oft regardless of Thy love,
Ungrateful, can from Thee depart,
  And from the path of duty rove.

4 Seal my forgiveness in the blood
  Of Christ my Lord; His Name alone
I plead for pardon, gracious God,
  And kind acceptance at Thy throne.

5 With hope in Him mine eyelids close;
  With sleep refresh my feeble frame;
Safe in Thy care may I repose,
  And wake with praises to Thy Name.

Anne Steele.

2 Swift to its close ebbs out life's little day;
Earth's joys grow dim, its glories pass away;
Change and decay in all around I see;
O Thou who changest not, abide with me!

3 I need Thy presence every passing hour;
What but Thy grace can foil the tempter's power?
Who like Thyself my guide and stay can be?
Through cloud and sunshine, O abide with me!

4 Hold Thou Thy cross before my closing eyes,
Shine through the gloom, and point me to the skies;
Heaven's morning breaks, and earth's vain shadows flee;
In life, in death, O Lord, abide with me!

Henry Francis Lyte.

Evening Worship

HURSLEY. L. M. — Peter Ritter, arr. by W. H. Monk.

Sun of my soul! Thou Saviour dear, It is not night if Thou be near:

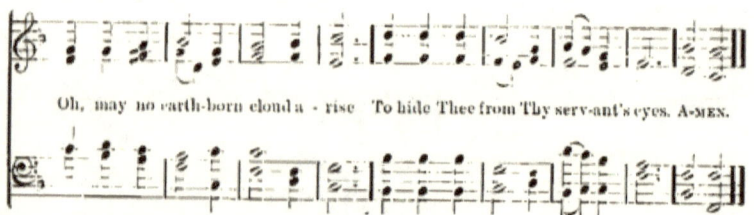

Oh, may no earth-born cloud arise To hide Thee from Thy servant's eyes. A-MEN.

10

Sun of my soul! Thou Saviour dear,
It is not night if Thou be near:
O may no earth-born cloud arise
To hide Thee from Thy servant's eyes

2 When the soft dews of kindly sleep
My weary eyelids gently steep,
Be my last thought—how sweet to rest
For ever on my Saviour's breast!

3 Abide with me from morn till eve,
For without Thee I cannot live;
Abide with me when night is nigh,
For without Thee I dare not die.

4 Be near to bless me when I wake,
Ere through the world my way I take,
Abide with me till in Thy love
I lose myself in heaven above.

John Keble.

11

AGAIN, as evening's shadow falls,
We gather in these hallowed walls;
And evening hymn and evening prayer
Rise mingling on the holy air.

2 May struggling hearts, that seek release,
Here find the rest of God's own peace;
And, strengthened here by hymn and prayer,
Lay down the burden and the care.

3 O God our Light, to Thee we bow;
Within all shadows standest Thou:
Give deeper calm than night can bring,
Give sweeter songs than life can sing.

4 Life's tumult we must meet again
We cannot at the shrine remain;
But in the spirit's secret cell,
May hymn and prayer forever dwell.

Samuel Longfellow.

12

Saviour, breathe an evening blessing.
  Ere repose our spirits seal;
Sin and want we come confessing,
  Thou can'st save, and Thou can'st heal.
Though destruction walk around us,
  Though the arrows past us fly,
Angel guards from Thee surround us,
  We are safe if Thou art nigh.

2 Though the night be dark and dreary,
  Darkness cannot hide from Thee;
Thou art He who, never weary,
  Watchest where Thy people be.
Should swift death this night o'ertake us,
  And our couch become our tomb,
When the judgment-day shall wake us,
  May we rise in deathless bloom.

James Edmeston.

Evening Worship.

TALLIS' CANON. L. M.   Thomas Tallis.

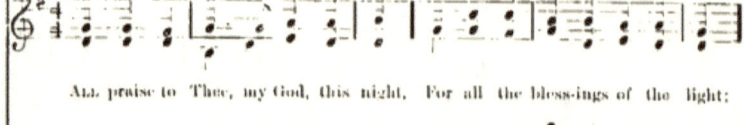

All praise to Thee, my God, this night, For all the bless-ings of the light;

Keep me, O keep me, King of kings, Be-neath Thine own Almighty wings! A - men.

13

2 Forgive me, Lord, for Thy dear Son,
The ill that I this day have done;
That with the world, myself, and Thee,
I, ere I sleep, at peace may be.

3 Teach me to live, that I may dread
The grave as little as my bed;
To die, that this vile body may
Rise glorious at the awful day.

4 O when shall I, in endless day,
For ever chase dark sleep away,
And hymns divine with angels sing
In endless praise to Thee, my King?

5 Praise God, from whom all blessings flow,
Praise Him, all creatures here below;
Praise Him above, ye heavenly host;
Praise Father, Son, and Holy Ghost.
               Thomas Ken.

14

Thus far the Lord has led me on;
  Thus far His power prolongs my days;
And every evening shall make known
  Some fresh memorial of His grace.

2 Much of my time has run to waste,
  And I, perhaps, am near my home,
But He forgives my follies past,
  And gives me strength for days to come.

3 I lay my body down to sleep;
  Peace is the pillow for my head;
While well-appointed angels keep
  Their watchful stations round my bed.

4 Thus when the night of death shall come,
  My flesh shall rest beneath the ground,
And wait Thy voice to break my tomb,
  With sweet salvation in the sound.
               Isaac Watts.

Evening Worship.

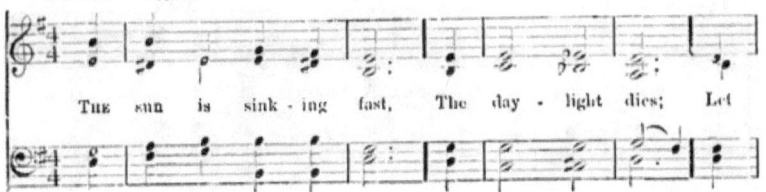

SUNSET. 3,4,5,6. S. G. Potts.

The sun is sink-ing fast, The day-light dies; Let love a-wake and pay ...... Her eve-ning sac-ri-fice. A-MEN.

15

2 As Christ upon the cross
  His head inclined,
And to His Father's hands
  His parting soul resigned.

3 So now herself my soul
  Would wholly give
Into His sacred charge,
  In Whom all spirits live;

4 So now beneath His eye
  Would calmly rest,
Without a wish or thought
  Abiding in the breast.

5 Thus would I live: yet now
  Not I, but He,
In all His power and love,
  Henceforth alive in me.
      Tr. Edward Caswall.

16

ANOTHER day is past;
  'Tis evening-tide;
O may Thy blessing, Lord,
  Within our hearts abide.

2 Another day is past,
  Of prayer and praise;
And once again to Thee
  Our grateful hearts we raise.

3 Another day is past:
  And still Thy love,
Like evening's balmy dew,
  Is falling from above.

4 O keep us in Thy care,
  Dear Lord, we pray,
Till evening brings a morn
  That ne'er shall pass away.
      Fanny J. Crosby.

Opening of Service.

LIEBSTER JESU, WIR SIND HIER. 7,8,8.   Johann R. Ahle.

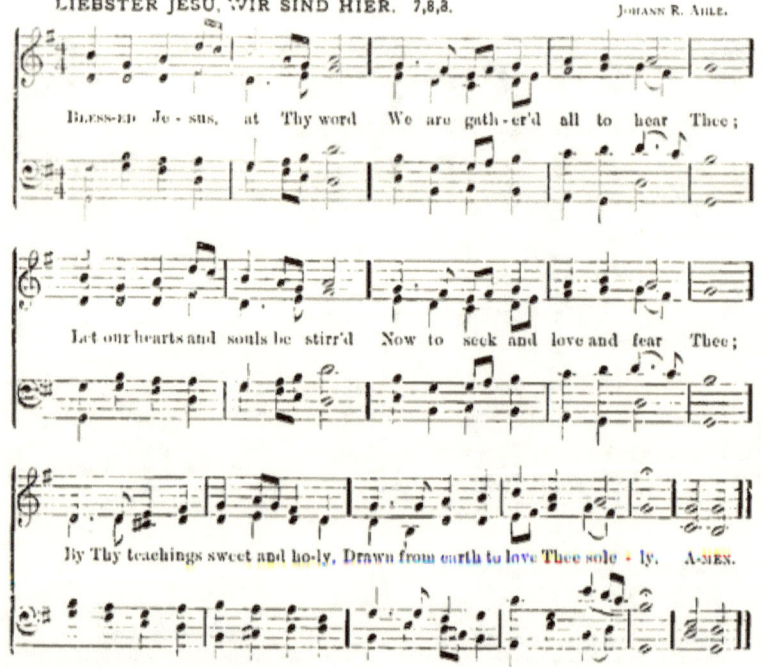

17

Blessed Jesus, at Thy word
 We are gathered all to hear Thee;
Let our hearts and souls be stirred
 Now to seek and love and fear Thee;
By Thy teachings sweet and holy,
Drawn from earth to love Thee solely.

2 All our knowledge, sense, and sight
 Lie in deepest darkness shrouded,
Till Thy Spirit breaks our night
 With the beams of truth unclouded.
Thou alone to God canst win us,
Thou must work all good within us.

3 Glorious Lord, Thyself impart!
 Light of light, from God proceeding,
Open Thou our ears and heart,
 Help us by Thy Spirit's pleading,
Hear the cry Thy people raises,
Hear, and bless our prayers and praises.

Tobias Clausnitzer.   Tr. Catherine Winkworth.

Opening of Service. 13

HERR JESU CHRIST, DICH ZU UNS WEND. L. M.

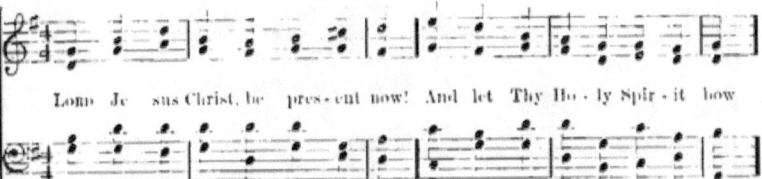

Lord Jesus Christ, be present now! And let Thy Holy Spirit bow

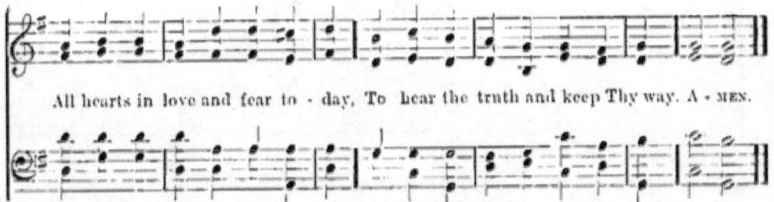

All hearts in love and fear to-day, To hear the truth and keep Thy way. A-MEN.

18

LORD Jesus Christ, be present now!
And let Thy Holy Spirit bow
All hearts in love and fear to-day,
To hear the truth and keep Thy way

2 Open our lips to sing Thy praise,
Our hearts in true devotion raise,
Strengthen our faith, increase our light,
That we may know Thy name aright:

3 Until we join the host that cry
"Holy art Thou, O Lord most High!"
And 'mid the light of that blest place,
Shall gaze upon Thee face to face,

4 Glory to God, the Father, Son,
And Holy Spirit, Three in one!
To Thee, O blessed Trinity,
Be praise throughout eternity!

Wm. August. H., Tr. Catherine Winkworth.

19

ALL people that on earth do dwell,
Sing to the Lord with cheerful voice:
Him serve with mirth, His praise forth tell,
Come ye before Him and rejoice.

2 Know that the Lord is God indeed,
Without our aid He did us make:
We are His flock, He doth us feed,
And for His sheep He doth us take.

3 Oh, enter then His gates with praise,
Approach with joy His courts unto:
Praise, laud, and bless His name always,
For it is seemly so to do.

4 For why? the Lord our God is good,
His mercy is for ever sure;
His truth at all times firmly stood,
And shall from age to age endure.

William Kethe.

Opening of Service.

ITALIAN HYMN. 6,4. FELICE GIARDINI.

Come, Thou Al-might-y King, Help us Thy name to sing, Help us to praise: Fa-ther! all-glo-ri-ous, O'er all vic-to-ri-ous, Come, and reign o-ver us, An-cient of Days! A-men

20

Come, Thou Almighty King,
Help us Thy name to sing,
 Help us to praise:
Father! all-glorious,
O'er all victorious,
Come, and reign over us,
 Ancient of Days!

2 Come, Thou incarnate Word,
Gird on Thy mighty sword;
 Our prayer attend:
Come, and Thy people bless,
And give Thy word success,
Spirit of holiness!
 On us descend.

3 Come, holy Comforter!
Thy sacred witness bear,
 In this glad hour:
Thou, who almighty art,
Now rule in every heart,
And ne'er from us depart,
 Spirit of power!

4 To the great One in Three
The highest praises be,
 Hence evermore!
His sovereign majesty
May we in glory see,
And to eternity
 Love and adore.

Charles Wesley.

Opening of Service.

HENDON. 7.   César H. A. Malan.

Lord, we come be-fore Thee now, At Thy feet we humbly bow; Oh, do not our suit dis-dain! Shall we seek Thee, Lord, in vain? Shall we seek Thee, Lord, in vain? Amen.

21

2 Lord, on Thee our souls depend,
In compassion now descend:
Fill our hearts with Thy rich grace,
Tune our lips to sing Thy praise.

3 In Thine own appointed way,
Now we seek Thee; here we stay;
Lord, we know not how to go,
Till a blessing Thou bestow.

4 Comfort those who weep and mourn;
Let the time of joy return:
Those that are cast down lift up;
Make them strong in faith and hope.

5 Grant that all may seek and find
Thee a God supremely kind;
Heal the sick; the captive free;
Let us all rejoice in Thee.
                        William Hammond.

22

Sweet the time, exceeding sweet!
When the saints together meet,
When the Saviour is the theme,
When they joy to sing of Him.

2 Sing we then eternal love,
Such as did the Father move:
He beheld the world undone,
Loved the world and gave His Son.

3 Sing the Son's amazing love;
How He left the realms above,
Took our nature and our place,
Lived and died to save our race.

4 Sing we, too, the Spirit's love;
With our stubborn hearts He strove,
Filled our minds with grief and fear,
Brought the precious Saviour near.
                        George Burder.

Opening of Service.

UNSER HERRSCHER, UNSER KÖNIG. 8,7,7.   Joachim Neander.

O-pen now thy gates of beau-ty, Zi-on, let me en-ter there,
Where my soul, in joy-ful du-ty, Waits for Him who an-swers pray'r;
O how bless-ed is this place, Filled with sol-ace, light, and grace! A-MEN.

2 Yes, my God, I come before Thee,
  Come Thou also down to me;
Where we find Thee and adore Thee
  There a heaven on earth must be.
To my heart O enter Thou,
Let it be Thy temple now.

3 Here Thy praise is gladly chanted,
  Here Thy seed is duly sown;
Let my soul, where it is planted,
  Bring forth precious sheaves alone,
So that all I hear may be
Fruitful unto life in me.

4 Thou my faith increase and quicken,
  Let me keep Thy gift divine,
Howsoe'er temptations thicken,
  May Thy Word still o'er me shine;
As my pole-star through my life,
As my comfort in my strife.

5 Speak, O God, and I will hear Thee,
  Let Thy will be done indeed;
May I undisturbed draw near Thee
  While Thou dost Thy people feed;
Here of life the fountain flows,
Here is balm for all our woes.

Benjamin Schmolck. Tr. Catherine Winkworth.

Closing of Service.

SCHUMANN. S. M.   Robert Schumann.

Once more, be-fore we part, Oh, bless the Sav-iour's name!

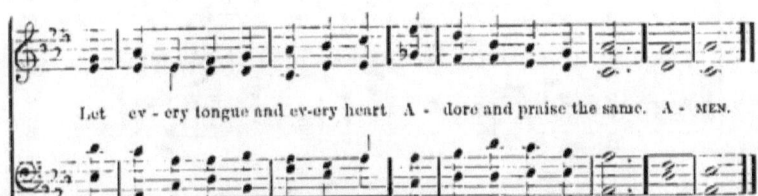

Let ev-ery tongue and ev-ery heart A-dore and praise the same. A-MEN.

24
Once more, before we part,
  Oh, bless the Saviour's name!
Let every tongue and every heart
  Adore and praise the same.

2 Lord, in Thy grace we came,
  That blessing still impart;
We met in Jesus' sacred name,
  In Jesus' name we part.

3 Still on Thy holy word
  Help us to feed and grow,
Still to go on to know the Lord,
  And practice what we know.

4 Now, Lord, before we part,
  Help us to bless Thy name;
Let every tongue and every heart
  Adore and praise the same.
                Joseph Hart.

25
The swift declining day,
  How fast its moments fly!
While evening's broad and gloomy shade
  Gains on the western sky.

2 Ye mortals, mark its pace,
  And use the hours of light;
And know, its Maker can command
  At once eternal night.

3 Give glory to the Lord,
  Who rules the whirling sphere;
Submissive at His footstool bow,
  And seek salvation there.

4 Then shall new lustre break
  Through death's impending gloom,
And lead you to unchanging light,
  In your celestial home.
                Philip Doddridge.

Closing of Service.

SICILIAN MARINERS' HYMN. 8,7,4.　　　MARCANTOINE PORTOGALLO.

Lord, dismiss us with Thy blessing, Fill our hearts with joy and peace!
Let us each, Thy love possessing, Triumph in redeeming grace.
O refresh us, O refresh us, Travelling thro' this wilderness. A-MEN.

26

Lord, dismiss us with Thy blessing,
  Fill our hearts with joy and peace!
Let us each, Thy love possessing,
  Triumph in redeeming grace.
      O refresh us,
  Travelling through this wilderness.

2 Thanks we give and adoration
  For Thy Gospel's joyful sound:
May the fruits of Thy salvation
  In our hearts and lives abound.
      May Thy presence
  With us evermore be found.

3 So, whene'er the signal's given
    Us from earth to call away,
  Borne on angels' wings to heaven,
    Glad the summons to obey,
        May we, ready,
    Rise and reign in endless day.

Walter Shirley.

Closing of Service.

ELLERS. 10. Edward J. Hopkins.

Saviour, again to Thy dear name we raise
With one accord our parting hymn of praise;
Once more we bless Thee ere our worship cease,
Then, lowly bending, wait Thy word of peace. A-MEN.

27

2 Grant us Thy peace upon our homeward way;
With Thee began, with Thee shall end the day;
Guard Thou the lips from sin, the hearts from shame,
That in this house have called upon Thy name.

3 Grant us Thy peace, Lord, through the coming night,
Turn Thou for us its darkness into light;
From harm and danger keep Thy children free,
For dark and light are both alike to Thee.

4 Grant us Thy peace throughout our earthly life,
Our balm in sorrow, and our stay in strife;
Then, when Thy voice shall bid our conflict cease,
Call us, O Lord, to Thine eternal peace.

John Ellerton

Closing of Service.

ILKLEY. 8,7,7. JAMES W. ELLIOTT.

Saviour, now the day is end-ing, And the shades of eve-ning fall;
Let the Ho-ly Ghost, de-scend-ing, Bring Thy mer-cy to us all.
Set Thy seal on ev-'ry heart, Je-sus! bless us ere we part. A-MEN.

28

2 Bless the Gospel-message, spoken
   In Thine own appointed way;
Give each longing soul a token
   Of Thy tender love to-day.
Set Thy seal on every heart,
Jesus! bless us ere we part.

3 Comfort those in pain and sorrow,
   Watch each sleeping child of Thine;
Let us all arise to-morrow
   Strengthened by Thy grace divine;
Set Thy seal on every heart,
Jesus! bless us ere we part.

4 Pardon Thou each deed unholy;
   Lord, forgive each sinful thought;
Make us contrite, pure, and lowly,
   By Thy great example taught:
Set Thy seal on every heart,
Jesus! bless us ere we part.

                      Sarah Doudney.

Closing of Service.

ARUNDEL. 8,7.
John B. Dykes.

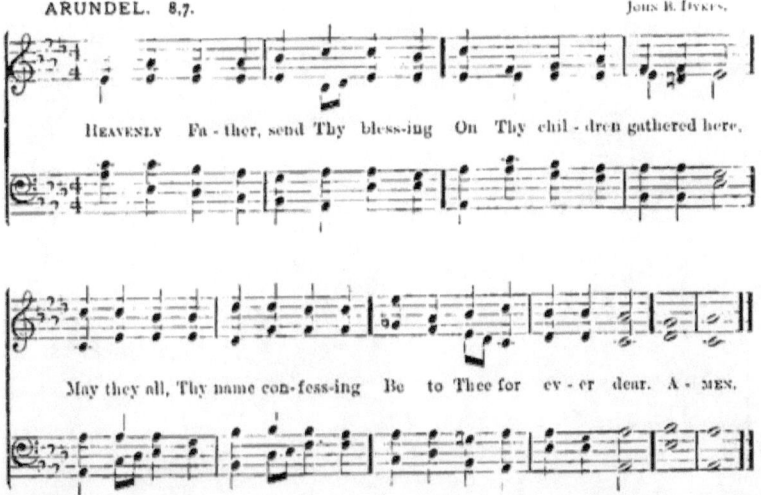

Heavenly Fa-ther, send Thy bless-ing On Thy chil-dren gathered here.

May they all, Thy name con-fess-ing Be to Thee for ev-er dear. A-men.

29

Heavenly Father, send Thy blessing
 On Thy children gathered here,
May they all, Thy name confessing,
 Be to Thee for ever dear.

2 May they be like Joseph, loving,
 Dutiful, and chaste, and pure;
And their faith, like David, proving,
 Steadfast unto death endure.

3 Holy Saviour, Who in meekness
 Didst vouchsafe a Child to be,
Guide their steps and help their weakness,
 Bless and make them like to Thee.

4 Spread Thy golden pinions o'er them,
 Holy Spirit, from above;
Guide them, lead them, go before them,
 Give them peace, and joy and love.

5 Temples of the Holy Spirit,
 May they with Thy glory shine,
And immortal bliss inherit,
 And for evermore be Thine.
   Christopher Wordsworth.

30

Saviour! all my sins confessing,
 Gracious hear me when I cry;
Give, thro' faith, the promised blessing,
 Freely, fully *justify*.

2 By Thy Holy Spirit's leading,
 Bring me to Thy bosom nigh;
In Thy blessed footsteps treading
 Soul and body *sanctify*.

3 So, the days of conflict ended,
 In the mansions of the sky,
Whither, Lord, Thou art ascended,
 With Thyself, me *glorify*.
   Thomas Haweis.

Closing of Service.

TALLIS' CANON. L. M. — Thomas Tallis

Sweet Saviour, bless us ere we go; Thy Word in-to our minds in-still; And make our luke-warm hearts to glow With low-ly love and fer-vent will. A-MEN.

31

2 The day is done, its hours have run,
   And Thou hast taken count of all;
The scanty triumphs grace hath won,
   The broken vow, the frequent fall.

3 Grant us, dear Lord, from evil ways
   True absolution and release;
And bless us more than in past days
   With purity and inward peace.

4 Do more than pardon: give us joy,
   Sweet fear and sober liberty,
And loving hearts without alloy,
   That only long to be like Thee.

5 For all we love, the poor, the sad,
   The sinful, unto Thee we call:
O let Thy mercy make us glad!
   Thou art our Jesus and our All.

Frederic W. Faber.

32

LORD, now we part in Thy blest name,
In which we here together came;
Grant us, our few remaining days,
To work Thy will, and spread Thy praise.

2 Teach us in life and death to bless
Thee, Lord, our strength and righteousness
Grant that we all may meet above,
Where we shall better sing Thy love.

3 Dismiss us with Thy blessing, Lord;
Help us to feed upon Thy word;
All that has been amiss forgive,
And let Thy truth within us live.

4 To God the Father, God the Son,
And God the Spirit, Three in One,
Be honor, praise, and glory given,
By all on earth, and all in heaven.

Ver. 1, 2, 4 - John Dracup. Ver 3 - Joseph Hart.

Prayer.

HORTON. 7.   VON DER SCHNYDER

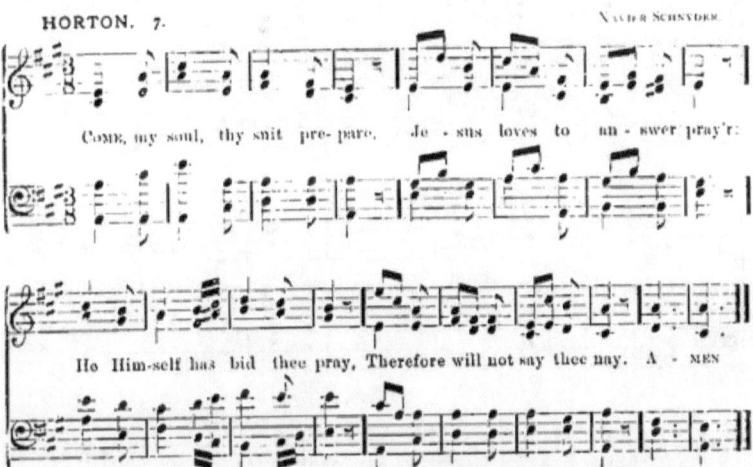

Come, my soul, thy suit pre-pare. Je-sus loves to an-swer pray'r:
He Him-self has bid thee pray, Therefore will not say thee nay. A-MEN

33

2 Thou art coming to a King;
Large petitions with thee bring;
For His grace and power are such,
None can ever ask too much.

3 With my burden I begin;
Lord, remove this load of sin!
Let Thy Blood, for sinners spilt,
Set my conscience free from guilt.

4 Lord, I come to Thee for rest!
Take possession of my breast;
There Thy blood-bought right maintain,
And without a rival reign.

5 While I am a pilgrim here,
Let Thy love my spirit cheer;
As my Guide, my Guard, my Friend,
Lead me to my journey's end.

6 Show me what I have to do,
Every hour my strength renew;
Let me live a life of faith,
Let me die Thy people's death.
John Newton.

34

Lord! I cannot let Thee go,
Till a blessing Thou bestow;
Do not turn away Thy face,
Mine's an urgent, pressing case.

2 Once a sinner, near despair,
Sought Thy mercy-seat by prayer;
Mercy heard and set him free—
Lord! that mercy came to me.

3 Many days have passed since then,
Many changes I have seen;
Yet have been upheld till now,
Who could hold me up but Thou?

4 Thou hast helped in every need—
This emboldens me to plead;
After so much mercy past,
Canst Thou let me sink at last?

5 No—I must maintain my hold;
'Tis Thy goodness makes me bold;
I can no denial take,
Since I plead for Jesus' sake.
John Newton.

Prayer.

RIPLEY. 8,7. D.   LOWELL MASON.

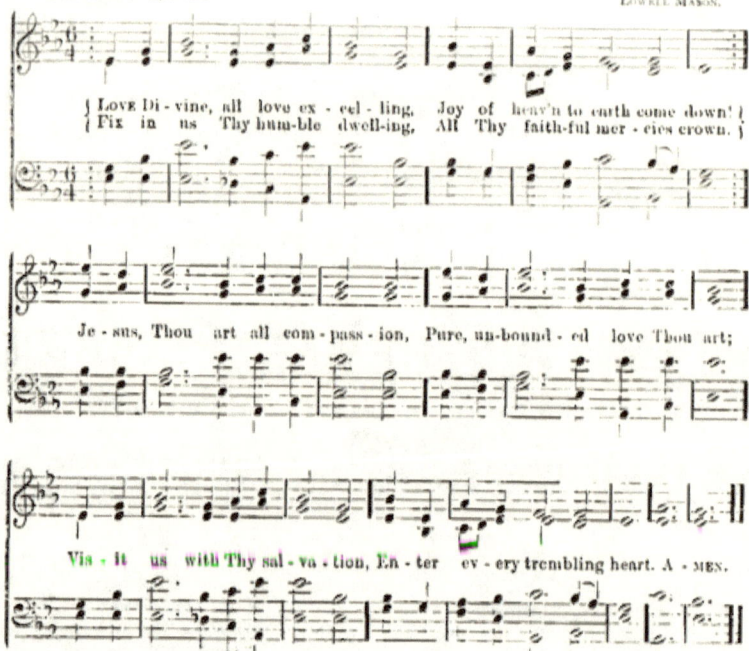

Love Di-vine, all love ex-cel-ling, Joy of heav'n to earth come down!
Fix in us Thy hum-ble dwell-ing, All Thy faith-ful mer-cies crown.
Je-sus, Thou art all com-pass-ion, Pure, un-bound-ed love Thou art;
Vis-it us with Thy sal-va-tion, En-ter ev-ery trembling heart. A-MEN.

35

2 Breathe, O breathe Thy loving Spirit
   Into every troubled breast!
Let us all in Thee inherit,
   Let us find Thy promised rest.
Take away the love of sinning,
   Alpha and Omega be;
End of faith, as its beginning,
   Set our hearts at liberty.

3 Come, Almighty to deliver,
   Let us all Thy life receive;
Graciously return, and never,
   Never more Thy temples leave!

Thee we would be always blessing,
   Serve Thee as Thy hosts above,
Pray and praise Thee without ceasing,
   Glory in Thy precious love.

4 Finish then Thy new creation,
   Pure and spotless let us be;
Let us see Thy great salvation
   Perfectly restored in Thee!
Changed from glory into glory,
   Till in heaven we take our place,
Till we cast our crowns before Thee,
   Lost in wonder, love, and praise.

                                     Charles Wesley.

prayer.

MANOAH. C. M.   FRANZ J. HAYDN.

Lord, teach us how to pray a-right, With rev-'rence and with fear: Though dust and ash-es in Thy sight, We may, we must draw near. A-MEN.

36

2 Burdened with guilt, convinced of sin,
  In weakness, want, and woe,
Fightings without and fears within,
  Lord, whither shall we go?

3 God of grace, we come to Thee
  With broken, contrite hearts;
Give, what Thine eye delights to see,
  Truth in the inward parts.

4 Give deep humility; the sense
  Of godly sorrow give;
A strong desire, with confidence,
  To hear Thy voice and live.

5 Give these, and then Thy will be done;
  Thus strengthened with all might,
We, through Thy Spirit and Thy Son,
  Shall pray, and pray aright.
                James Montgomery.

37

LORD! when we bend before Thy throne,
  And our confessions pour,
Oh, may we feel the sins we own,
  And hate what we deplore.

2 Our contrite spirits pitying see;
  True penitence impart:
And let a healing ray from Thee
  Beam hope on every heart.

3 When we disclose our wants in prayer,
  May we our wills resign;
Nor let a thought our bosom share,
  Which is not wholly Thine.

4 Let faith each meek petition fill,
  And waft it to the skies;
And teach our heart 'tis goodness still
  That grants it or denies.
                Joseph D. Carlyle.

Prayer.

DIJON. 7.   Johann G. Bitthauer.

Stealing from the world away, We are come to seek Thy face;

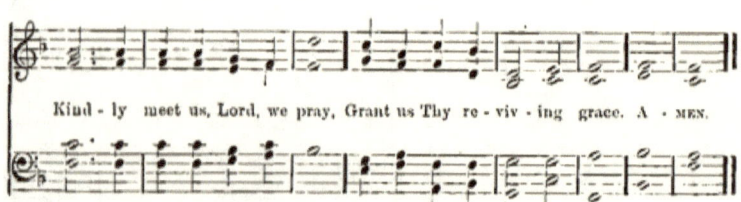

Kindly meet us, Lord, we pray, Grant us Thy reviving grace. A-men.

38

Stealing from the world away,
  We are come to seek Thy face;
Kindly meet us, Lord, we pray,
  Grant us Thy reviving grace.

2 Yonder stars that gild the sky
  Shine but with a borrowed light;
We, unless Thy light be nigh,
  Wander, wrapt in gloomy night.

3 Sun of Righteousness! dispel
  All our darkness, doubts and fears;
May Thy light within us dwell,
  Till eternal day appears.

4 Warm our hearts in prayer and praise,
  Lift our every thought above;
Hear the grateful songs we raise,
  Fill us with Thy perfect love.
    Ray Palmer.

39

To Thy pastures fair and large,
Heavenly Shepherd, lead Thy charge,
And my couch, with tenderest care,
'Mid the springing grass prepare.

2 When I faint with summer's heat,
Thou shalt guide my weary feet
To the streams that, still and slow,
Through the verdant meadows flow.

3 Safe the dreary vale I tread,
By the shades of death o'erspread,
With Thy rod and staff supplied,
This my guard—and that my guide.

4 Constant to my latest end,
Thou my footsteps shalt attend;
And shalt bid Thy hallowed dome
Yield me an eternal home.
    James Merrick.

Prayer.

CHRISTUS DER IST MEIN LEBEN. 7,6.   Fr. Melchior Vulpius.

A-bide with us, our Saviour, Nor let Thy mercy cease;
From Satan's might defend us, And grant our souls release. A-MEN.

40

ABIDE with us, our Saviour,
  Nor let Thy mercy cease;
From Satan's might defend us,
  And grant our souls release.

2 Abide with us, our Saviour,
  Sustain us by Thy Word;
That we with all Thy people
  To life may be restored.

3 Abide with us, our Saviour,
  Thou Light of endless light;
Increase to us Thy blessings,
  And save us by Thy might.

4 To Father, Son, and Spirit,
  Eternal One and Three,
As was, and is for ever,
  And praise and glory be.

Nicholaus Selnecker, tr.

41

LORD Jesus, by Thy passion,
  To Thee I make my prayer;
Thou Who in mercy smitest,
  Have mercy, Lord, and spare.

2 Oh, wash me in the fountain
  That floweth from Thy side!
Oh, clothe me in the raiment
  Thy blood hath purified!

3 Oh, hold Thou up my goings,
  And lead from strength to strength,
That unto Thee in Sion
  I may appear at length!

4 Oh, make my spirit worthy
  To join that ransomed throng!
Oh, teach my lips to utter
  That everlasting song!

Richard F. Littledale.

Praise.

ALLEIN GOTT IN DER HÖH' SEY EHR. 8,7. Iambic. JOHANN KUGELMANN.

All glory be to God on High, Who hath our race be-friend-ed!
To us no harm shall now come nigh, The strife at last is end-ed;
God show-eth His good will to men, And peace shall reign on
earth a-gain; Oh, thank Him for His good - ness. A-MEN.

42

2 We praise, we worship Thee, we trust,
 And give Thee thanks for ever,
O Father, that Thy rule is just,
 And wise, and changes never:
Thy boundless power o'er all things reigns,
Thou dost whate'er Thy will ordains;
 Well for us that Thou rulest!

3 O Jesus Christ, our God and Lord,
 Son of Thy Heavenly Father,
O Thou who hast our peace restored
 And the lost sheep dost gather,
Thou Lamb of God, to Thee on high
From out our depths we sinners cry.
 Have mercy on us, Jesus!

4 O Holy Ghost, Thou precious Gift,
 Thou Comforter unfailing,
O'er Satan's snares our souls uplift,
 And let Thy power availing
Avert our woes and calm our dread;
For us the Saviour's Blood was shed;
 We trust in Thee to save us!

Nicholas Decius (Von Hofe). Tr. Catherine Winkworth.

43
2 O may this bounteous God,
  Through all our life be near us,
With ever joyful hearts,
  And blessèd peace to cheer us;
And keep us in His grace,
  And guide us when perplexed,
And free us from all ills,
  In this world and the next.

3 All praise and thanks to God
  The Father, now be given,
The Son and Him who reigns
  With them in highest heaven;
The One eternal God,
  Whom earth and heaven adore;
For thus it was, is now,
  And shall be evermore!

Martin Rinkart. Tr., Catherine Winkworth.

PRAISE. 6,5. D.   THOMAS MORLEY.

Praise the Lord of heav-en, Praise Him in the height, Praise Him, all ye an-gels, Praise Him, stars and light; Praise Him, clouds and waters, Which a-bove the skies, When His word com-mand-ed, Did es-tab-lished rise. A-MEN.

44

Praise the Lord of heaven,
  Praise Him in the height,
Praise Him, all ye angels,
  Praise Him, stars and light:
Praise Him, clouds and waters,
  Which above the skies,
When His word commanded,
  Did established rise.

2 Praise the Lord, ye fountains
  Of the deeps and seas,
Rocks, and hills, and mountains,
  Cedars, and tall trees:

Praise, Him clouds and vapors,
  Snow, and hail, and fire,
Stormy winds, fulfilling
  Only His desire.

3 Praise Him, fowls and cattle,
  Princes and all kings;
Praise Him, men and maidens,
  All created things:
For the Name of God is
  Excellent alone,
Over earth His footstool,
  Over heaven His throne.

              Thomas B. Browne.

45

Praise to the Lord! the Almighty, the King of creation!
O my soul, praise Him, for He is thy health and salvation!
    All ye who hear,
      Now to His temple draw near,
        Join me in glad adoration.

2 Praise to the Lord! who o'er all things so wondrously reigneth,
Shelters thee under His wings, yea, so gently sustaineth;
    Hast thou not seen
      How thy desires e'er have been
        Granted in what He ordaineth?

3 Praise to the Lord! who doth prosper thy work and defend thee;
Surely His goodness and mercy here daily attend thee.
    Ponder anew
      What the Almighty can do,
        If with His love He befriend thee!

4 Praise to the Lord! O let all that is in me adore Him!
All that hath life and breath, come now with praises before Him!
    Let the Amen
      Sound from His people again;
        Gladly for aye we adore Him.

                      Joachim Neander. Tr. Catherine Winkworth.

OLD HUNDRED. L. M.

Louis Bourgeois.

Be-fore Je-ho-vah's aw-ful throne, Ye na-tions! bow with sa-cred joy:

Know that the Lord is God a-lone; He can cre-ate, and He de-stroy. A-MEN.

46

2 His sovereign power, without our aid,
  Made us of clay, and formed us men;
And when, like wandering sheep, we stray'd,
  He brought us to His fold again.

3 We are His people, we His care,—
  Our souls, and all our mortal frame;
What lasting honors shall we rear,
  Almighty Maker! to Thy name?

4 We'll crowd Thy gates with thankful songs,
  High as the heavens our voices raise;
And earth, with her ten thousand tongues,
  Shall fill Thy courts with sounding praise.

5 Wide as the world is Thy command,
  Vast as eternity, Thy love;
Firm as a rock Thy truth must stand,
  When rolling years shall cease to move.

  Isaac Watts.

47

With one consent let all the earth
  To God their cheerful voices raise;
Glad homage pay with awful mirth,
  And sing before Him songs of praise.

2 Convinced that He is God alone,
  From Whom both we and all proceed;
We, whom He chooses for His own,
  The flock that He vouchsafes to feed.

3 Oh, enter then His temple gate,
  Thence to His courts devoutly press;
And still your grateful hymns repeat,
  And still His Name with praises bless.

4 For He's the Lord, supremely good,
  His mercy is forever sure;
His truth, which always firmly stood,
  To endless ages shall endure.

  Tate & Brady.

48

2 Dwelleth the light of the glory with Him,
Light of a glory that cannot grow dim,
Light in its silence and beauty and calm,
Light in its gladness and brightness and balm.

3 Ever ascendeth the song and the joy,
Ever descendeth the love from on high,
Blessing, and honor, and glory, and praise,
This is the theme of the hymns that we raise.

4 Life of all life, and true Light of all light,
Star of the dawning, unchangingly bright,
Sun of the Salem whose lamp is the Lamb,
Theme of the ever-new, ever-glad psalm!

5 Give we the glory and praise to the Lamb,
Take we the robe and the harp and the psalm,
Sing we the song of the Lamb that was slain,
Dying in weakness, but rising to reign.

Horatius Bonar.

praise.

SILVER STREET. S. M.
Isaac Smith.

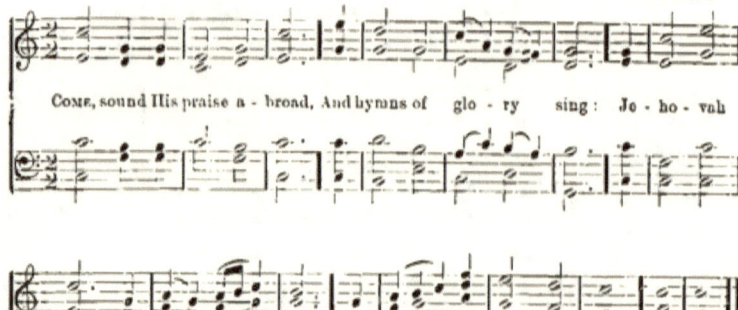

Come, sound His praise a-broad, And hymns of glo-ry sing: Jehovah is the sov-'reign God, The u-ni-ver-sal King. A-men.

49

Come, sound His praise abroad,
  And hymns of glory sing:
Jehovah is the sovereign God,
  The universal King.

2 He formed the deeps unknown;
  He gave the seas their bound;
The watery worlds are all His own,
  And all the solid ground.

3 Come, worship at His throne,
  Come, bow before the Lord:
We are His work, and not our own,
  He formed us by His word.

4 To-day attend His voice,
  Nor dare provoke His rod;
Come, like the people of His choice,
  And our own gracious God.
Isaac Watts.

50

O bless the Lord, my soul!
  Let all within me join,
And aid my tongue to bless His Name,
  Whose favors are divine.

2 O bless the Lord, my soul!
  Nor let His mercies lie
Forgotten in unthankfulness,
  And without praises die.

3 'Tis He forgives thy sins;
  'Tis He relieves thy pain;
'Tis He that heals thy sicknesses,
  And gives thee strength again.

4 He crowns thy life with Love,
  When ransomed from the grave;
He that redeemed my soul from death
  Hath sovereign power to save
Isaac Watts.

Praise. 35

LYONS. 10,11. Franz J. Haydn.

O wor-ship the King all-glo-rious a-bove, And grate-ful-ly sing His won-der-ful love; Our Shield and De-fend-er, the An-cient of Days. Pa-villioned in splendor, and gird-ed with praise. A-MEN.

51

2 O tell of His might, and sing of His grace,
Whose robe is the light, whose canopy space;
His chariots of wrath the deep thunder-clouds form,
And dark is His path on the wings of the storm.

3 Thy bountiful care what tongue can recite?
It breathes in the air, it shines in the light,
It streams from the hills, it descends to the plain,
And sweetly distills in the dew and the rain.

4 Frail children of dust, and feeble as frail,
In Thee do we trust, nor find Thee to fail;
Thy mercies how tender! how firm to the end!
Our Maker, Defender, Redeemer, and Friend.

Robert Grant.

2 O Holy Father, Who hast led Thy children
   In all the ages, with the Fire and Cloud,
Through seas dry-shod; through weary wastes bewildering;
   To Thee, in reverent love, our hearts are bowed.

3 O Holy Jesus, Prince of Peace and Saviour,
   To Thee we owe the peace that still prevails,
Stilling the rude wills of men's wild behaviour,
   And calming passion's fierce and stormy gales.

William C. Doane.

Praise.

PARK STREET. L. M.   Frederick M. A. Venua.

O come, loud anthems let us sing, Loud thanks to our almighty King, And high our grateful voices raise, As our Salvation's Rock we praise, As our Salvation's Rock we praise. A-MEN.

53
2 Into His presence let us haste
To thank Him for His favors past;
To Him address, in joyful songs,
The praise that to His name belongs.

3 For God the Lord, enthroned in state,
Is with unrivalled glory great;
The depths of earth are in His hand,
Her secret wealth at His command.

4 Oh, let us to His courts repair,
And bow with adoration there;
Low on our knees with reverence fall,
And on the Lord our Maker, call.
                        Tate & Brady.

54
Triumphant Zion! lift thy head
From dust, and darkness, and the dead!
Though humbled long—awake at length,
And gird thee with thy Saviour's strength!

2 No more shall foes unclean invade,
And fill thy hallowed walls with dread;
No more shall hell's insulting host
Their victory and thy sorrows boast.

3 God from on high has heard thy prayer,
His hand thy ruins shall repair;
Nor will thy watchful Monarch cease
To guard thee in eternal peace.
                        Philip Doddridge.

FABEN. 8,7. D.   JOHN H. WILLCOX.

Lord, Thy glory fills the heaven; Earth is with its fullness stored;
Unto Thee be glory given, Holy, Holy, Holy Lord!
Heav'n is still with anthems ringing; Earth takes up the angels' cry;
"Holy, Holy, Holy," singing, "Lord of hosts, Thou Lord most high!" A-MEN.

55

2 Ever thus in God's high praises,
  Brethren, let our tongues unite,
While our thoughts His greatness raises,
  And our love His gifts excite;
With His seraph train before Him
  With His holy Church below,
Thus unite we to adore Him,
  Bid we thus our anthem flow:

3 "Lord, Thy glory fills the heaven:
  Earth is with its fullness stored;
Unto Thee be glory given,
  Holy, Holy, Holy Lord!"
Thus, Thy glorious day confessing,
  We adopt the angels' cry,
"Holy, Holy, Holy!" blessing
  Thee, the Lord our God most high!
                Richard Mant.

56

We give immortal praise
To God the Father's love,
For all our comforts here,
And all our hopes above:
He sent His own Eternal Son
To die for sins that man had done.

2 To God the Son belongs
Immortal glory too,
Who bought us with His blood
From everlasting woe;
And now He lives, and now He reigns
And sees the fruit of all His pains.

3 To God the Spirit praise
And endless worship give,
Whose new-creating power
Makes the dead sinner live:
His work completes the great design
And fills the soul with joy divine.

4 Almighty God, to Thee
Be endless honors done,
The Sacred Persons Three,
The Godhead only One:
Where reason fails with all her powers
There faith prevails, and love adores.

Isaac Watts

Praise.

ROSEFIELD. 7.   Cæsar H. A. Malan.

Ho-ly, ho-ly, ho-ly Lord! Be Thy glo-rious name a-dor'd:

Lord, Thy mercies nev-er fail; Hail, co-les-tial Goodness, hail! A-men.

57
Holy, holy, holy Lord!
Be Thy glorious name adored;
Lord, Thy mercies never fail;
Hail, celestial Goodness, hail!

2 Though unworthy, Lord, Thine ear
Deign our humble songs to hear;
Purer praise we hope to bring,
When around Thy throne we sing.

3 There no tongue shall silent be;
All shall join in harmony;
That through heaven's capacious round
Praise to Thee may ever sound.

4 Lord, Thy mercies never fail;
Hail, celestial Goodness, hail!
Holy, holy, holy Lord!
Be Thy glorious name adored.
                Benjamin Williams.

58
Sing, my soul, His wondrous love,
Who, from yon bright throne above,
Ever watchful of our race,
Still to man extends His grace.

2 Heaven and earth by Him were made;
All is by His sceptre swayed;
What are we that He should show
So much love to us below?

3 God, the merciful and good,
Bought us with the Saviour's blood;
And, to make our safety sure,
Guides us by His Spirit pure.

4 Sing, my soul, adore His name!
Let His glory be thy theme;
Praise Him till He calls thee home;
Trust His love for all to come.
                Anon.

59

2 Holy, Holy, Holy! all the saints adore Thee,
  Casting down their golden crowns around the glassy sea;
Cherubim and Seraphim falling down before Thee,
  Which wert, and art, and evermore shalt be.

3 Holy, Holy, Holy! though the darkness hide Thee,
  Though the eye of sinful man Thy glory may not see,
Only Thou art Holy; there is none beside Thee
  Perfect in power, in love, and purity.

4 Holy, Holy, Holy! Lord God Almighty!
  All Thy works shall praise Thy name, in earth, and sky, and sea;
Holy, Holy, Holy. Merciful and Mighty;
  God in Three Persons, Blessèd Trinity!

Reginald Heber.

60

Father, who the light this day
  Out of darkness didst create,
Shine upon us now, we pray,
  While within Thy courts we wait.
Wean us from the works of night,
Make us children of the light.

2 Saviour, who this day didst break
  From the bondage of the tomb,
Bid our slumbering souls awake;
  Shine through all their sin and gloom;
Let us, from our bonds set free,
Rise from sin, and live to Thee.

3 Blessèd Spirit, Comforter,
  Sent this day from Christ on high;
Lord, on us Thy gifts confer,
  Cleanse, illumine, sanctify;
All Thine influence shed abroad;
Lead us to the truth of God.

Julia A. Elliott.

The Lord's Day.

SABBATH. 7, 6 lines.   LOWELL MASON.

Safe-ly through an-oth-er week, God has brought us on our way;
Let us now a bless-ing seek, Wait-ing in His courts to-day:
Day of all the week the best, Em-blem of e-ter-nal rest;
Day of all the week the best, Em-blem of e-ter-nal rest. A-MEN.

61

2 Mercies multiplied each hour
   Through the week, our praise demand;
Guarded by Thy mighty power,
   Fed and guided by Thy hand;
Though ungrateful we have been,
Only made returns of sin.

3 While we pray for pardoning grace,
   Through the dear Redeemer's name,
Show Thy reconciling face,
   Take away our sin and shame:
From our worldly cares set free,
May we rest this day in Thee.

4 May the Gospel's joyful sound
   Conquer sinners, comfort saints;
Make the fruits of grace abound,
   Bring relief for all complaints.
Thus may all our Sabbaths prove,
Till we join the Church above.

                                                  John Newton.

The Lord's Day.

DAY OF REST. 7,6. D.   JOSEPH BARNBY.

O day of rest and gladness, O day of joy and light,
O balm of care and sadness, Most beautiful, most bright;
On thee, the high and lowly, Through ages joined in tune,
Sing, Holy, Holy, Holy! To the great God Triune. A-MEN.

62

2 On thee, at the creation,
   The light first had its birth;
On thee for our salvation
   Christ rose from depths of earth;
On thee our Lord victorious
   The Spirit sent from heaven;
And thus on thee most glorious
   A triple light was given.

3 Thou art a port protected
   From storms that round us rise;
A garden intersected
   With streams of Paradise;
Thou art a cooling fountain
   In life's dry, dreary sand;
From thee, like Pisgah's mountain,
   We view our promised land.

The Lord's Day.

4 To-day on weary nations
  The heavenly manna falls;
To holy convocations
  The silver trumpet calls,
Where gospel light is glowing
  With pure and radiant beams,
And living water flowing
  With soul-refreshing streams.

5 New graces ever gaining
  From this our day of rest,
We reach the Rest remaining
  To spirits of the blest.
To Holy Ghost be praises,
  To Father, and to Son;
The Church her voice upraises
  To Thee, blest Three in One.
Christopher Wordsworth.

BELMONT. C. M. William Gardiner.

Blest day of God! most calm, most bright, The first, the best of days;
The laborer's rest, the saint's de-light, The day of pray'r and praise. A-men.

63

2 My Saviour's face made thee to shine;
  His rising thee did raise,
And made thee heavenly and divine
  Beyond all other days.

3 The first-fruits oft a blessing prove
  To all the sheaves behind;
And they the day of Christ who love,
  A happy week shall find.

4 This day I must with God appear;
  For, Lord, the day is Thine;
Help me to spend it in Thy fear,
  And thus to make it mine.
John Mason.

The Lord's Day.

MIGDOL. L. M.   LOWELL MASON.

How pleasant, how divinely fair, O Lord of hosts, Thy dwellings are!
With long desire my spirit faints, To meet th' assemblies of Thy saints. A-MEN.

64

2 My flesh would rest in Thine abode,
My panting heart cries out for God;
My God! my King! why should I be
So far from all my joys, and Thee?

3 Blest are the saints who sit on high,
Around Thy throne of majesty;
Thy brightest glories shine above,
And all their work is praise and love.

4 Blest are the souls who find a place
Within the temple of Thy grace;
There they behold Thy gentler rays,
And seek Thy face, and learn Thy praise.

5 Cheerful they walk with growing strength,
Till all shall meet in heaven at length;
Till all before Thy face appear,
And join in nobler worship there.
Isaac Watts.

65

This day the light, of heavenly birth,
First streamed upon the new-born earth;
O Lord, this day upon us shine,
And fill our souls with light divine.

2 This day the Saviour left the grave,
And rose, omnipotent to save;
O Jesus, may we raiséd be
From death of sin to life in Thee.

3 This day the Holy Spirit came,
With fiery tongues of cloven flame;
O Spirit, fill our hearts this day
With grace to hear, and grace to pray.

4 O day of Light, and Life, and Grace!
From earthly toils sweet resting-place;
Thy hallowed hours, best gift of love,
We give again to God above.
William W. How.

The Lord's Day.

MORGENGLANZ DER EWIGKEIT. 7, 6 lines.

66

Jesus, Sun of Righteousness,
  Brightest beam of love divine,
With the early morning rays
  Do Thou on our darkness shine,
And dispel with purest light
All our long and gloomy night!

2 Like the sun's reviving ray,
  May Thy Love with tender glow,
All our coldness melt away,
  Warm and cheer us forth to go,
Gladly serve Thee and obey
All our life's short earthly day!

3 Thou our only Hope and Guide!
  Never leave us, nor forsake:
In Thy light may we abide
  Till the endless morning break;
Moving on to Zion's hill,
Onward, upward, homeward still!

4 Lead us all our days and years
  In Thy straight and narrow way,
Lead us through the vale of tears
  To the land of perfect day,
Where Thy people, fully blest,
Near Thy throne for ever rest.

Christian Knorr. *Tr.* Jane Borthwick.

The Lord's Day.

MONTGOMERY. 7.
FREDERICK A. G. OUSELEY.

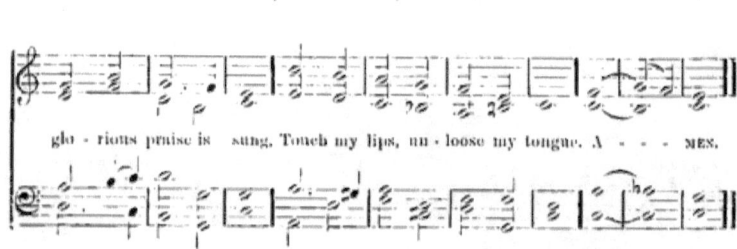

67

2 While the prayers of saints ascend,
God of love, to mine attend;
Hear me, for Thy Spirit pleads;
Hear, for Jesus intercedes.

3 While I hearken to Thy law,
Fill my soul with humble awe,
Till Thy Gospel bring to me
Life and immortality.

4 While Thy ministers proclaim
Peace and pardon in Thy Name,
Through their voice, by faith, may I
Hear Thee speaking from the sky.

5 From Thy house when I return,
May my heart within me burn;
And at evening let me say,
"I have walked with God to-day."

James Montgomery.

68

PLEASANT are Thy courts above,
In the land of light and love;
Pleasant are Thy courts below,
In this land of sin and woe.

2 O, my spirit longs and faints
For the converse of Thy saints,
For the brightness of Thy face,
For Thy fulness, God of grace!

3 Happy souls! their praises flow
Even in this vale of woe;
Waters in the desert rise,
Manna feeds them from the skies:

4 On they go from strength to strength,
Till they reach Thy throne at length,
At Thy feet adoring fall,
Who has led them safe through all.

Henry F. Lyte.

The Lord's Day.

CADWELL. S. M. — William W. Rousseau

Welcome, sweet day of rest, That saw the Lord a rise; Welcome to this re-viv-ing breast, And these re-joic-ing eyes. A-MEN.

69

Welcome, sweet day of rest,
  That saw the Lord arise;
Welcome to this reviving breast,
  And these rejoicing eyes.

2 The King Himself comes near
  And feasts His saints to-day;
Here may we seek, and see Him here,
  And love, and praise, and pray.

3 One day of prayer and praise
  His sacred courts within,
Is sweeter than ten thousand days
  Of pleasurable sin.

4 My willing soul would stay
  In such a frame as this,
And wait to hail the brighter day
  Of everlasting bliss.
            Isaac Watts.

70

This is the day of light,
  Let there be light to-day;
O Dayspring, rise upon our night,
  And chase its gloom away.

2 This is the day of rest,
  Our failing strength renew!
On weary brain and troubled breast
  Shed Thou Thy fresh'ning dew.

3 This is the day of peace,
  Thy peace our spirits fill;
Bid Thou all ill and discord cease,
  The waves of strife be still.

4 This is the day of prayer,
  Let earth to heaven draw near;
Lift up our hearts to seek Thee there,
  Come down to meet us here.
            John Ellerton.

Advent.

MACHT HOCH DIE THUR. 8,6.

Lift up your heads, ye mighty gates! Behold the King of glory waits;
The King of kings is drawing near, The Saviour of the world is here;
Life and salvation He doth bring, Wherefore rejoice, and gladly sing:
We praise Thee, Father, now, Creator, wise art Thou! A-men.

71

2 The Lord is just, a Helper tried,
Mercy is ever at His side;
His kingly crown is holiness,
His sceptre, pity in distress,
The end of all our woe He brings;
Wherefore the earth is glad and sings:
  We praise Thee, Saviour, now,
  Creator, wise art Thou!

3 O blest the land, the city blest,
Where Christ the Ruler is confest!
O happy hearts and happy homes
To whom this King in triumph comes!
The cloudless Sun of joy He is,
Who bringeth pure delight and bliss:
  O Comforter Divine,
  What boundless grace is Thine!

Advent.   51

4 Fling wide the portals of your heart;
Make it a temple, set apart
From earthly use for heaven's employ,
Adorned with prayer, and love, and joy;
So shall your Sovereign enter in,
And new and nobler life begin:
  To Thee, O God, be praise,
  For word and deed and grace!

5 Redeemer, come! I open wide
My heart to Thee; here, Lord, abide!
Let me Thy inner presence feel,
Thy grace and love in me reveal;
Thy Holy Spirit guide us on,
Until our glorious goal be won!
  Eternal praise and fame
  We offer to Thy name.
George Weissel. *Tr.* Catherine Winkworth.

GOTT SEI DANK DURCH ALLE WELT. 7.   1704.

Let the earth now praise the Lord, Who hath tru-ly kept His word,
And the sin-ner's Help and Friend Now at last to us doth send. A-MEN.

72

2 What the fathers most desired,
What the prophets' heart inspired,
What they longed for many a year
Stands fulfilled in glory here.

3 Abram's promised great reward,
Zion's Helper, Jacob's Lord,
Him of twofold race behold,
Truly come, as long foretold.

4 Welcome, O my Saviour, now!
Hail! my Portion, Lord, art Thou!
Here too in my heart, I pray,—
O prepare Thyself a way.

5 And when Thou dost come again,
As a glorious King to reign,
I with joy may see Thy face,
Freely ransomed by Thy grace.
Henry Held. *Tr.* Catherine Winkworth.

73

Come, Thou long-expected Jesus,
  Born to set Thy people free;
From our fears and sins release us,
  Let us find our rest in Thee.
Israel's Strength and Consolation,
  Hope of all the earth Thou art;
Dear Desire of every nation,
  Joy of every longing heart.

2 Born Thy people to deliver;
  Born a Child, and yet a King;
Born to reign in us for ever,
  Now Thy gracious kingdom bring.
By Thine own eternal Spirit,
  Rule in all our hearts alone;
By Thine all-sufficient merit,
  Raise us to Thy glorious throne.
                        Charles Wesley.

Advent.

WEBB. 7,6. D. George Webb.

Hail to the Lord's Anointed, Great David's greater Son! Hail, in the time appointed, His reign on earth begun! He comes to break oppression, To set the captive free, To take away transgression, And rule in equity. A-MEN.

74

2 He comes, with succor speedy,
  To those who suffer wrong;
To help the poor and needy,
  And bid the weak be strong;
To give them songs for sighing,
  Their darkness turn to light,
Whose souls, condemned and dying,
  Were precious in His sight.

3 He shall come down like showers
  Upon the fruitful earth,
And love, and joy, like flowers,
  Spring in His path to birth:
Before Him, on the mountains,
  Shall peace the herald go,
And righteousness in fountains
  From hill to valley flow.

4 For Him shall prayer unceasing
  And daily vows ascend;
His kingdom still increasing,
  A kingdom without end.
The heavenly dew shall nourish
  A seed in weakness sown,
Whose fruit shall spread and flourish,
  And shake like Lebanon.

5 O'er every foe victorious,
  He on His throne shall rest;
From age to age more glorious,
  All-blessing and all-blessed.
The tide of time shall never
  His covenant remove;
His name shall stand for ever;
  His great, best name of Love!

James Montgomery.

CHRISTMAS. C. M. GEORGE F. HANDEL.

A-rise, the king-dom is at hand, The King is draw-ing nigh; A-rise with

joy, thou faithful band, To meet the Lord most high! To meet the Lord most high! AMEN.

75

2 Look up, ye souls weighed down with care,
   The Sovereign is not far;
Look up, faint hearts, from your despair,
   Behold the Morning Star!

3 Now fear and wrath to joy give place,
   Now are our sorrows o'er,
Since God hath made us in His grace
   His children evermore.

4 O rich the gifts Thou bringest us,
   Thyself made poor and weak;
O Love beyond compare that thus
   Can foes and sinners seek!

5 For this we raise a gladsome voice
   On high to Thee alone,
And evermore with thanks rejoice
   Before Thy glorious throne.

John Rist. *Tr.* Catherine Winkworth.

76

MORTALS! awake, with angels join,
   And chant the solemn lay;
Joy, love, and gratitude, combine
   To hail th' auspicious day.

2 In heaven the rapturous song began,
   And sweet seraphic fire
Through all the shining regions ran,
   And strung and tuned the lyre.

3 Swift, through the vast expanse, it flew;
   And loud the echo rolled;
The theme, the song, the joy was new,
   'Twas more than heaven could hold.

4 With joy the chorus we repeat—
   "Glory to God on high:"
Good-will and peace are now complete:
   Jesus was born to die.

Samuel Medley.

Advent.

FREU' DICH SEHR. 8,7,7,8.

Com-fort, com-fort ye my peo-ple, Speak ye peace, thus saith our God;
Com-fort those who sit in dark-ness, Mourning 'neath their sor-rows' load;
Speak ye to.... Je-ru-sa-lem Of the peace that waits for them.
Tell her that her sins I cov-er, And her war-fare now is o-ver. A-MEN.

77

2 For the Herald's voice is crying
  In the desert far and near,
Bidding all men to repentance,
  Since the kingdom now is here.
O that warning cry obey!
Now prepare for God a way!
Let the valleys rise to meet Him,
And the hills bow down to greet Him

3 Make ye straight what long was crooked,
  Make the rougher places plain:
Let your hearts be true and humble,
  As befits His holy reign;
For the glory of the Lord
Now o'er earth is shed abroad,
And all flesh shall see the token,
That His word is never broken.

John Olearius (Oelschlager). Tr. Catherine Winkworth.

ANTIOCH. C. M.   George F. Handel.

78

Joy to the world, the Lord is come!
    Let earth receive her King;
Let every heart prepare Him room,
    And heaven and nature sing.

2 Joy to the earth; the Saviour reigns;
    Let men their songs employ;
While fields and floods, rocks, hills, and plains,
    Repeat the sounding joy.

3 No more let sins and sorrows grow,
    Nor thorns infest the ground;
He comes to make His blessings flow
    Far as the curse is found.

4 He rules the world with truth and grace,
    And makes the nations prove
The glories of His righteousness,
    And wonders of His love.

                        Isaac Watts.

Advent.

79
Lo! He comes with clouds descending,
  Once for our salvation slain;
Thousand angel-hosts attending:
  Swell the triumph of His train:
    Alleluia!
  Christ the Lord returns to reign.

2 Every eye shall now behold Him,
  Robed in dreadful majesty;
Those who set at naught and sold Him,
  Pierced, and nailed Him to the tree,
    Deeply wailing,
  Shall the true Messiah see.

3 Now redemption, long expected,
  See in solemn pomp appear:
All His saints, by men rejected,
  Now shall meet Him in the air:
    Alleluia!
  See the day of God appear.

4 Yea, Amen; let all adore Thee,
  High on Thine eternal throne;
Saviour, take the power and glory;
  Claim the kingdoms for Thine own:
    Alleluia!
  Thou shalt reign, and Thou alone.
      John Cennick. Charles Wesley. Martin M. Madan.

ST. THEODULPH. 7,6. D.
Advent.
MELCHIOR TESCHNER.

O how shall I receive Thee, How greet Thee, Lord, aright?
All nations long to see Thee, My hope, my heart's delight!
O kindle, Lord, most holy, Thy lamp within my breast,
To do in spirit lowly All that may please Thee best. A-MEN.

80

2 Thy Zion palms is strewing,
   And branches fresh and fair;
My heart, its powers renewing,
   An anthem shall prepare.
My soul puts off her sadness
   Thy glories to proclaim;
With all her strength and gladness
   She fain would serve Thy name.

3 Rejoice then, ye sad-hearted,
   Who sit in deepest gloom,
Who mourn o'er joys departed,
   And tremble at your doom:
He who alone can cheer you,
   Is standing at the door;
He brings His pity near you,
   And bids you weep no more.

Paul Gerhardt.

81

REJOICE, all ye believers,
   And let your lights appear!
The evening is advancing,
   And darker night is near.
The Bridegroom is arising,
   And soon He draweth nigh.
Up! pray, and watch, and wrestle—
   At midnight comes the cry!

2 Our Hope and Expectation,
   O Jesus, now appear;
Arise, Thou Sun so longed for,
   O'er this benighted sphere!
With hearts and hands uplifted,
   We plead, O Lord, to see
The day of earth's redemption,
   That brings us unto Thee!

Laurentius Laurenti. Tr. Jane Borthwick.

Advent.

OH COME, EMMANUEL. 8, 6 lines.

Oh come, oh come, Emmanuel, And ransom captive Israel;
That mourns in lonely exile here, Until the Son of God appear.
Rejoice! rejoice! Emmanuel Shall come to thee, O Israel! A-MEN.

82

2 O come, Thou Rod of Jesse, free
Thine own from Satan's tyranny;
From depths of hell Thy people save,
And give them victory o'er the grave.—*Cho.*

3 O come, Thou Day-Spring, come and cheer
Our spirits by Thine Advent here:
And drive away the shades of night,
And pierce the clouds, and bring us light!—*Cho.*

4 O come, Thou Key of David, come,
And open wide our heavenly home;
Make safe the way that leads on high,
And close the path to misery.—*Cho.*

Tr John M. Neale.

ADESTE FIDELES. 11.   Christmas.   MARC ANTOINE PORTOGALLO.

83
2 True Son of the Father, He comes from the skies;
To be born of a Virgin He does not despise;
To Bethlehem hasten, with joyful accord;
O come ye, come hither, to worship the Lord!

3 To Thee, then, O Jesus, this day of Thy birth,
Be glory and honor through heaven and earth.
True Godhead incarnate, omnipotent Word!
O come, let us hasten to worship the Lord!

Edward Caswall.

84

2 "To you, in David's town, this day
  Is born of David's line,
The Saviour, Who is Christ the Lord:
  And this shall be the sign:
The heavenly Babe you there shall find
  To human view displayed,
All meanly wrapt in swathing bands,
  And in a manger laid."

3 Thus spake the seraph; and forthwith
  Appeared a shining throng
Of angels praising God, who thus
  Addressed their joyful song:
"All glory be to God on high,
  And to the earth be peace;
Good-will henceforth from heaven to men
  Begin and never cease."

Nahum Tate.

Christmas.

VOM HIMMEL HOCH. L. M.

Good news from heav'n the an-gels bring, Glad ti-dings to the earth they sing: To us this day a Child is giv'n, To crown us with the joy of heav'n. A-MEN.

85

2 This is the Christ, our God and Lord,
Who in all need shall aid afford;
He will Himself our Saviour be,
From all our sins to set us free.

3 To us that blessédness He brings,
Which from the Father's bounty springs:
That in the heavenly realm we may
With Him enjoy eternal day.

4 Ah, dearest Jesus, holy Child,
Make Thee a bed, soft, undefiled,
Within my heart, that it may be
A quiet chamber kept for Thee.

5 Praise God upon His heavenly throne,
Who gave to us His only Son:
For this His hosts, on joyful wing,
A blest New Year of mercy sing.

Martin Luther.   Tr. Catherine Winkworth.

SILENT NIGHT! P. M.   Franz Gruber.

Si-lent night! Ho-ly night! All is calm, all is bright, Round yon Vir-gin

Christmas.

Glories stream from Heaven afar,
Heav'nly hosts sing Alleluia,
Christ, the Saviour, is born!

3 Silent night! Holy night!
Son of God, love's pure light
Radiant, beams from Thy holy Face
With the dawn of redeeming grace,
Jesus, Lord, at Thy birth.

Tr. Joseph Mohr.

86

2 Silent night! Holy night!
Shepherds quake at the sight!

87

2 Within a manger He doth lie,
Whose throne is set above the sky.

3 Stillness was all the manger round,
The creature its Creator found.

4 The wise men came, led by the star,
Gold, myrrh, and incense brought from far.

5 His mother is the Virgin mild,
And He the Father's only Child.

Anon.

Christmas.

SEARS. C. M. D.   A. A. Wild.

It came up-on the mid-night clear, That glo-rious song of old,
From an-gels bend-ing near the earth To touch their harps of gold;
Peace on the earth, good will to men, From heav'n's all-gra-cious King;
The world in sol-emn still-ness lay To hear the an-gels sing. A-men.

Used by permission.

88

2 Still through the cloven skies they come,
   With peaceful wings unfurled;
And still their heavenly music floats
   O'er all the weary world;
Above its sad and lonely plains
   They bend on hovering wing,
And ever o'er its Babel sounds
   The blessèd angels sing.

3 For lo, the days are hastening on,
   By prophets seen of old,
When with the ever-circling years,
   Shall come the time foretold,
When the new heaven and earth shall owe
   The Prince of Peace their King,
And the whole world send back the song
   Which now the angels sing.

Edmund H. Sears.

Christmas.

GERTRUDE. 8,7. George C. F. Haas.

Hark! what mean those ho-ly voic-es Sweet-ly sounding thro' the skies?

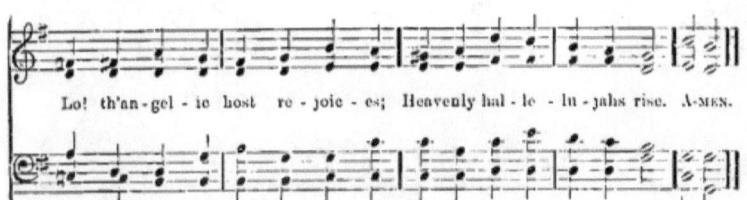

Lo! th'an-gel-ic host re-joic-es; Heavenly hal-le-lu-jahs rise. A-MEN.

89

2 Listen to the wondrous story,
 Which they chant in hymns of joy:
"Glory in the highest, glory!
 Glory be to God most high!

3 "Peace on earth, good-will from heaven,
 Reaching far as man is found;
Souls redeemed, and sins forgiven;
 Loud our golden harps shall sound.

4 "Hasten, mortals, to adore Him;
 Learn His name, and taste His joy;
Till in heaven ye sing before Him,
 Glory be to God most high!"

5 Let us learn the wondrous story
 Of our great Redeemer's birth;
Spread the brightness of His glory,
 Till it cover all the earth.
 John Cawood.

90

SHEPHERDS! hail the wondrous Stranger,
 Now to Bethlehem speed your way;
Lo! in yonder humble manger
 Christ, the Lord, is born to-day.

2 Bright the star of your salvation
 Pointing to His rude abode!
Rapturous news for every nation:—
 Mortals! now behold your God!

3 Glad, we trace th' amazing story
 Angels leave their bliss to tell;
Theme sublime, replete with glory,—
 Sinners saved from death and hell.

4 Love eternal moved the Saviour,
 Thus to lay His radiance by;
Blessings on the Lamb forever!
 Glory be to God on high!
 "Union Minstrel," 1844.

Epiphany.

DEVOTION. 8,7. — LIEUT. S. CARTER.

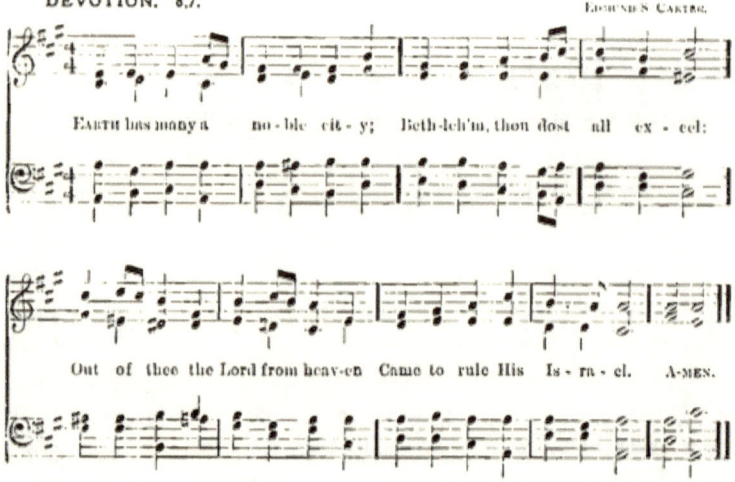

Earth has many a noble city; Beth-leh'm, thou dost all ex-cel: Out of thee the Lord from heav-en Came to rule His Is-ra-el. A-MEN.

91

2 Fairer than the sun at morning
  Was the star that told His birth,
To the world its God announcing
  Seen in fleshly form on earth.

3 Eastern sages at His cradle
  Make oblations rich and rare;
See them give, in deep devotion,
  Gold, and frankincense, and myrrh.

4 Sacred gifts of mystic meaning:
  Incense doth their God disclose,
Gold the King of kings proclaimeth,
  Myrrh His sepulchre foreshows.

5 Jesus, Whom the Gentiles worshipped
  At Thy glad Epiphany,
Unto Thee, with God the Father
  And the Spirit, glory be.
          Tr. Edward Caswell.

92

HAIL, Thou Source of every blessing
  Sovereign Father of mankind!
Gentiles now, Thy grace possessing,
  In Thy courts admission find.

2 Grateful now we fall before Thee,
  In Thy Church obtain a place;
Now by faith behold Thy glory,
  Praise Thy truth, adore Thy grace.

3 Hail, Thou all-inviting Saviour!
  Gentiles now their offerings bring;
In Thy temple seek Thy favor,
  Jesus Christ, our Lord and King.

4 May we, body, soul and spirit,
  Live devoted to Thy praise,
Glorious realms of bliss inherit,
  Grateful anthems ever raise.
         "*Stewart's Collection.*"

Epiphany.

93

AS WITH gladness men of old
Did the guiding star behold,
As with joy they hailed its light,
Leading onward, beaming bright;
So, most gracious Lord, may we
Evermore be led to Thee.

2 As with joyful steps they sped,
Saviour, to Thy manger bed,
There to bend the knee before
Thee whom heaven and earth adore;
So may we with willing feet
Ever seek the mercy-seat.

3 As they offered gifts most rare
At Thy cradle rude and bare,
So may we with holy joy,
Pure and free from sin's alloy,
All our costliest treasures bring,
Christ, to Thee our heavenly King.

4 Holy Jesus, every day
Keep us in the narrow way;
And, when earthly things are past,
Bring our ransomed souls at last
Where they need no star to guide,
Where no clouds Thy glory hide.

William C. Dix.

Epiphany.

O JESU CHRIST, MEIN LEBENS LICHT. L. M.

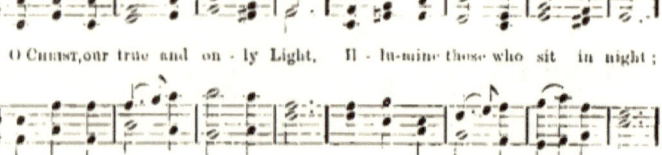

O Christ, our true and on-ly Light, Il-lu-mine those who sit in night;

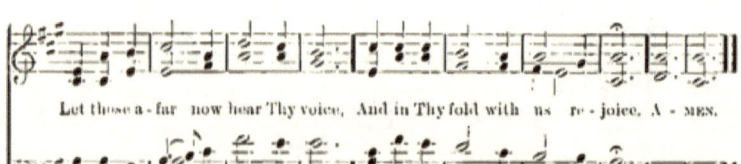

Let those a-far now hear Thy voice, And in Thy fold with us re-joice. A-MEN.

94

2 Fill with the radiance of Thy grace
The souls now lost in error's maze,
And all, O Lord, whose secret minds,
Some dark delusion hurts and blinds.

3 O make the deaf to hear Thy Word,
And teach the dumb to speak, dear Lord,
Who dare not yet the faith avow,
Though secretly they hold it now.

4 Shine on the darkened and the cold,
Recall the wanderers to Thy fold,
Unite those now who walk apart,
Confirm the weak and doubting heart.

5 So they with us may evermore
Such grace with wondering thanks adore,
And endless praise to Thee be given,
By all Thy Church in earth and heaven.

John Heermann. Tr. Catherine Winkworth.

95

LOOK from Thy sphere of endless day,
  O God of mercy and of might!
In pity look on those who stray,
  Benighted in this land of light.

2 Send forth Thy heralds, Lord, to call
  The thoughtless young, the hardened old,
A scattered, homeless flock, till all
  Be gathered to Thy peaceful fold.

3 Send them Thy mighty word to speak,
  Till faith shall dawn and doubt depart
To awe the bold, to stay the weak,
  And bind and heal the broken heart.

4 Then all these wastes, a dreary scene
  That makes us sadden as we gaze,
Shall grow with living waters green,
  And lift to heaven the voice of praise.

William C. Bryant.

Epiphany.

MANOAH. C. M. FRANZ J. HAYDN.

Bright was the guid-ing star that led, With mild, be-nig-nant ray, The Gen-tiles to the low-ly shed Where the Re-deem-er lay. A-MEN.

96

Bright was the guiding star that led,
  With mild, benignant ray,
The Gentiles to the lowly shed
  Where the Redeemer lay.

2 But, lo! a brighter, clearer light
  Now points to His abode;
It shines through sin and sorrow's night,
  To guide us to our God.

3 O haste to follow where it leads,
  His gracious call obey!
Be rugged wilds, or flowery meads,
  The Christian's destined way.

4 O gladly tread the narrow path,
  While light and grace are given!
For those who follow Christ on earth
  Shall reign with Him in heaven.
                          Harriet Auber.

97

O'er mountain-tops the mount of God
  In later days shall rise,
Above the summits of the hills,
  And draw the wond'ring eyes

2 To this the joyful nations round,
  All tribes and tongues, shall flow;
Up to the mount of God, they'll say,
  And to His house we'll go.

3 The beams that shine from Zion's hill
  Shall lighten every land;
The King who reigns in Salem's towers
  Shall all the world command.

4 Among the nations He shall judge;
  His judgments truth shall guide:
His sceptre shall protect the just,
  And crush the sinner's pride.
                          John Logan.

Epiphany.

FIAT LUX. 6,4. HENRY HILES.

Thou, whose al-might-y word Cha-os and dark-ness heard, And took their flight; Hear us, we hum-bly pray; And where the Gos-pel day Sheds not its glo-rious ray, Let there be light! A-MEN.

98

2 Thou, who didst come to bring,
On Thy redeeming wing,
  Healing and sight,
Health to the sick in mind,
Sight to the inly blind,
O, now to all mankind
  Let there be light!

3 Spirit of truth and love,
Life-giving, holy Dove,
  Speed forth Thy flight;
Move on the waters' face,
Bearing the lamp of grace,
And in earth's darkest place
  Let there be light!

4 Holy and blessed Three,
Glorious Trinity,
  Wisdom, Love, Might!
Boundless as ocean's tide
Rolling in fullest pride,
Through the earth, far and wide,
  Let there be light!

John Marriott.

Epiphany. 71

BRIGHTEST AND BEST. 11,10.

99
2 Cold on His cradle the dew-drops are shining,
 Low lies His head with the beasts of the stall;
Angels adore Him in slumber reclining,
 Maker and Monarch and Saviour of all.

3 Shall we not yield Him, in costly devotion,
 Odors of Edom, and offerings divine,
Gems of the mountain, and pearls of the ocean,
 Myrrh from the forest, and gold from the mine?

4 Vainly we offer each ample oblation,
 Vainly with gifts would His favor secure;
Richer by far is the heart's adoration,
 Dearer to God are the prayers of the poor.
                                    Reginald Heber.

72   Lent.

RATHBUN. 8,7.   ITHAMAR CONKEY.

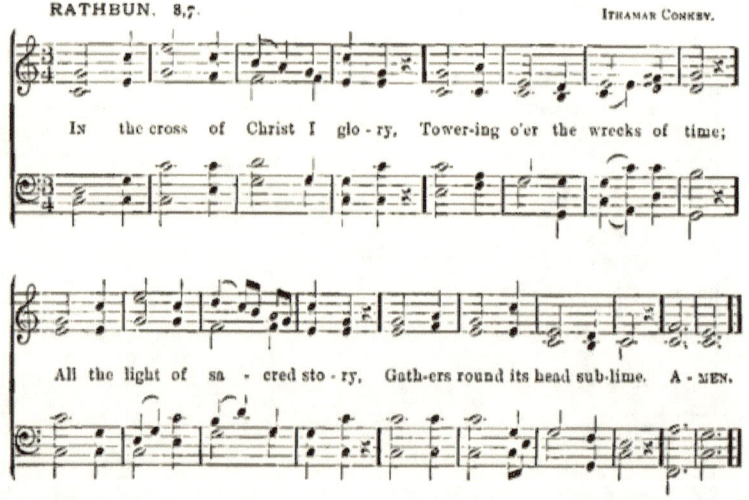

In the cross of Christ I glo-ry, Tower-ing o'er the wrecks of time;
All the light of sa-cred sto-ry, Gath-ers round its head sub-lime. A-MEN.

100

2 When the woes of life o'ertake me,
   Hopes deceive, and fears annoy,
Never shall the cross forsake me:
   Lo! it glows with peace and joy.

3 When the sun of bliss is beaming
   Light and love upon my way,
From the cross the radiance, streaming,
   Adds more lustre to the day.

4 Bane and blessing, pain and pleasure,
   By the cross are sanctified:
Peace is there, that knows no measure,
   Joys that through all time abide.

5 In the cross of Christ I glory,
   Towering o'er the wrecks of time;
All the light of sacred story,
   Gathers round its head sublime.
John Bowring.

101

STRICKEN, smitten and afflicted,
   See Him dying on the tree!
'Tis the Christ by man rejected;
   Yes, my soul, 'tis He! 'tis He!

2 Mark the Sacrifice appointed!
   See who bears the awful load;
'Tis the Word, the Lord's Anointed,
   Son of Man, and Son of God.

3 Here we have a firm foundation;
   Here the refuge of the lost;
Christ's the Rock of our salvation:
   His the Name of which we boast.

4 Lamb of God for sinners wounded!
   Sacrifice to cancel guilt!
None shall ever be confounded
   Who on Thee their hope have built.
Thomas Kelly.

Lent.

COWPER. C. M. *Lowell Mason.*

There is a fountain fill'd with blood Drawn from Emmanuel's veins; And sinners, plung'd be-neath that flood, Lose all their guilty stains, Lose all their guilty stains. A-MEN.

102

2 The dying thief rejoiced to see
  That fountain in his day;
And there may I, though vile as he,
  Wash all my sins away.

3 Dear dying Lamb, Thy precious blood
  Shall never lose its power,
Till all the ransomed Church of God
  Be saved to sin no more.

4 E'er since, by faith, I saw the stream
  Thy flowing wounds supply,
Redeeming love has been my theme,
  And shall be, till I die.

5 Then in a nobler, sweeter song,
  I'll sing Thy power to save,
When this poor lisping, stammering tongue
  Lies silent in the grave.
  William Cowper.

103

Alas! and did my Saviour bleed,
  And did my Sovereign die?
Would He devote that sacred Head
  For such a worm as I?

2 Well might the sun in darkness hide,
  And shut his glories in,
When God, the mighty Maker, died
  For man, the creature's sin!

3 Thus might I hide my blushing face,
  While His dear cross appears;
Dissolve my heart in thankfulness,
  And melt my eyes to tears.

4 But drops of grief can ne'er repay
  The debt of love I owe;
Here, Lord, I give myself away,
  'Tis all that I can do.
  Isaac Watts.

Lent.

HERZLICH THUT MICH VERLANGEN. 7,6. D.   Hans L. Hassler.

O sa-cred Head, now wound-ed, With grief and shame weigh'd down,
Now scorn-ful-ly sur-round-ed With thorns, Thy on-ly crown!
O sa-cred Head, what glo-ry, What bliss, till now, was Thine!
Yet, though despis'd and go-ry, I joy to call Thee mine. A-MEN.

104

2 How art Thou pale with anguish,
   With sore abuse and scorn!
How does that visage languish,
   Which once was bright as morn!
What Thou, my Lord, hast suffered,
   Was all for sinners' gain;
Mine, mine was the transgression,
   But Thine the deadly pain.

3 Lo, here I fall, my Saviour!
   'Tis I deserve Thy place!
Look on me with Thy favor,
   Vouchsafe to me Thy grace.
Receive me, my Redeemer;
   My Shepherd, make me Thine!
Of every good the Fountain,
   Thou art the Spring of mine!

4 What language shall I borrow
   To thank Thee, dearest Friend,
For this Thy dying sorrow,
   Thy pity without end!
O make me Thine for ever,
   And should I fainting be,
Lord, let me never, never,
   Outlive my love to Thee.

5 Forbid that I should leave Thee;
   O Jesus, leave not me;
In faith may I receive Thee,
   When death shall set me free.
When strength and comfort languish,
   And I must hence depart,
Release me then from anguish
   By Thine own wounded heart.

          Paul Gerhardt.   Tr. James W. Alexander.

Lent. 75

OLIVET. 6,4.   Lowell Mason.

My faith looks up to Thee, Thou Lamb of Cal-va-ry, Sav-iour di-vine; Now hear me while I pray; Take all my guilt a-way; Oh, let me from this day Be whol-ly Thine. A-men.

105

2 May Thy rich grace impart
Strength to my fainting heart,
  My zeal inspire;
As Thou hast died for me,
Oh, may my love to Thee
Pure, warm, and changeless be,
  A living fire.

3 While life's dark maze I tread,
And griefs around me spread,
  Be Thou my Guide;
Bid darkness turn to day,
Wipe sorrow's tears away,
Nor let me ever stray
  From Thee aside.

4 When ends life's transient dream,
When death's cold, sullen stream
  Shall o'er me roll;
Blest Saviour, then, in love,
Fear and distrust remove;
Oh, bear me safe above—
  A ransomed soul.

                              Ray Palmer.

106

2 Jesus, hail, enthroned in glory,
  There for ever to abide!
All the heavenly hosts adore Thee,
  Seated at Thy Father's side:
There for sinners Thou art pleading,
  There Thou dost our place prepare,
Ever for us interceding,
  Till in glory we appear.

3 Worship, honor, power and blessing,
  Thou art worthy to receive;
Loudest praises, without ceasing,
  Meet it is for us to give.
Help, ye bright angelic spirits,
  Bring your sweetest, noblest lays,
Help to sing our Saviour's merits,
  Help to chant Emmanuel's praise.

John Bakewell.

Lent.

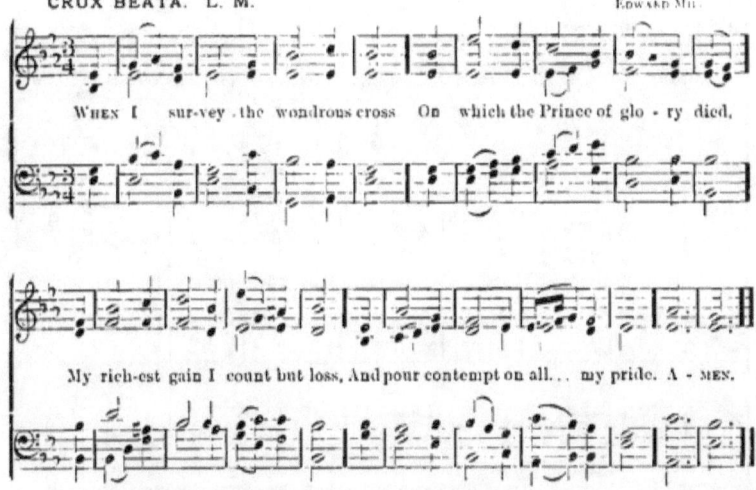

CRUX BEATA. L. M.   Edward Mil...

When I survey the wondrous cross On which the Prince of glo-ry died,
My rich-est gain I count but loss, And pour contempt on all... my pride. A-men.

107

When I survey the wondrous cross
On which the Prince of glory died,
My richest gain I count but loss,
And pour contempt on all my pride.

2 Forbid it, Lord, that I should boast,
Save in the cross of Christ, my God;
All the vain things that charm me most,
I sacrifice them to His blood.

3 See, from His head, His hands, His feet,
Sorrow and love flow mingled down!
Did e'er such love and sorrow meet?
Or thorns compose so rich a crown?

4 Were the whole realm of nature mine,
That were a tribute far too small;
Love so amazing, so divine,
Demands my soul, my life, my all.
                  Isaac Watts.

108

Awhile in spirit, Lord, to Thee
Into the desert would we flee;
Awhile upon the barren steep
Our fast with Thee in spirit keep.

2 Awhile from Thy temptation learn
False Satan's wileful lures to spurn;
And in our hearts to feel and own
"Man liveth not by bread alone."

3 O Thou once tempted like as we,
Thou knowest our infirmity;
Be Thou our helper in the strife,
Be Thou our true, our inward life.

4 And while at Thy command we pray
"Give us our bread from day to day,"
May we with Thee, O Christ, be fed,
Thou Word of God, Thou living Bread.
                  John F. Thrupp.

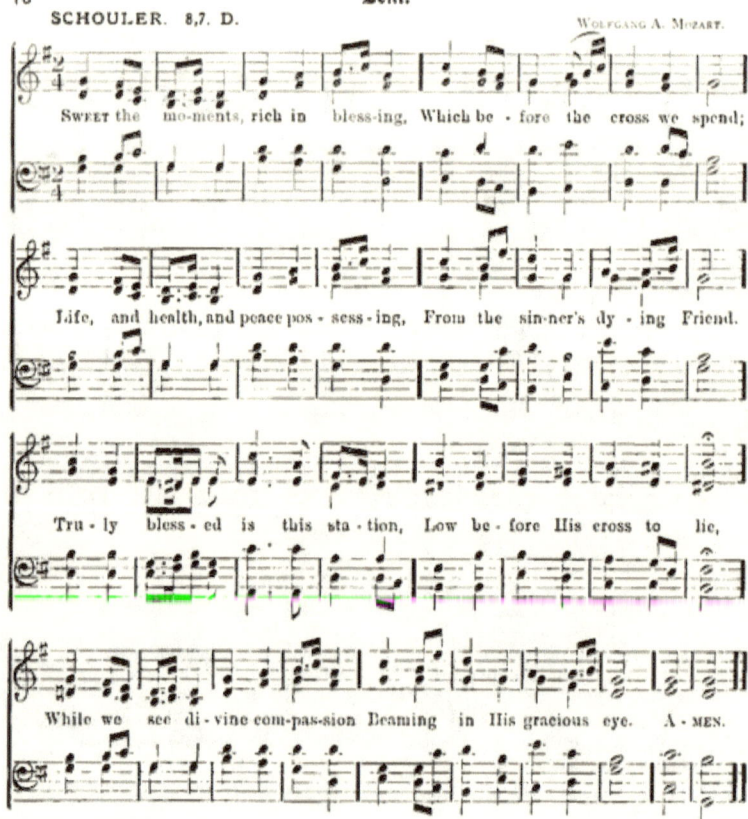

109

2 Love and grief our hearts dividing,
   With our tears His feet we bathe;
Constant still, in faith abiding,
   Life deriving from His death.
For Thy sorrows we adore Thee,
   For the pains that wrought our peace;
Gracious Saviour! we implore Thee
   In our souls Thy love increase.

3 Here we feel our sins forgiven,
   While upon the Lamb we gaze;
And our thoughts are all of heaven,
   And our lips o'erflow with praise.
Lord, in loving contemplation,
   Fix our hearts and eyes on Thee,
Till we taste Thy full salvation,
   And, unveiled, Thy glories see.

James Allen

Lent.

JESU, MEINES LEBENS LEBEN. 8,7,7.   1687.

Christ the Life of all the liv-ing, Christ the Death of death our foe,
Who Thyself for us once giv-ing To the dark-est depths of woe,
Pa-tient-ly didst yield Thy breath But to save my soul from death;
Thousand, thousand thanks shall be, Bless-ed Je-sus, un-to Thee. A-MEN.

110

2 Thou, ah Thou, hast taken on Thee
   Bitter strokes, a cruel rod;
Pain and scorn were heaped upon Thee,
   O Thou sinless Son of God.
Only thus for me to win
Rescue from the bonds of sin;
Thousand, thousand thanks shall be,
Blessed Jesus, unto Thee.

3 Thou didst bear the smiting only
   That it might not fall on me;
Stoodest falsely charged and lonely,
   That I might be safe and free;
Comfortless that I might know
Comfort from Thy boundless woe.
Thousand, thousand thanks shall be,
Blessed Jesus, unto Thee.

4 Then for all that wrought our pardon,
   For Thy sorrows deep and sore,
For Thine anguish in the garden,
   I will thank Thee evermore;
Thank Thee with my latest breath
For Thy sad and cruel death,
For that last and bitter cry:
Praise Thee evermore on high.

Ernst Christopher Homburg. Tr. Catherine Winkworth.

Easter.

STRAF MICH NICHT. 7, with Alleluia. GERMAN.

Christ the Lord is ris'n a-gain; Christ hath broken ev-ery chain; Hark, an-gel-ic voic-es cry, Singing ev-er-more on high, Al-le-lu-ia! A-MEN.

111

Christ the Lord is risen again;
Christ hath broken every chain;
Hark, angelic voices cry,
Singing evermore on high,   Alleluia!

2 He Who gave for us His life,
Who for us endured the strife,
Is our Paschal Lamb to-day;
We too sing for joy, and say   Alleluia!

3 He Who bore all pain and loss
Comfortless upon the cross,
Lives in glory now on high,
Pleads for us and hears our cry;   Alleluia!

4 He Who slumbered in the grave
Is exalted now to save;
Now through Christendom it rings
That the Lamb is King of kings.   Alleluia!
                    Michael Weiss. Tr. Catherine Winkworth.

112

Jesus Christ is risen to-day,
Our triumphant holy day,
Who did once upon the cross
Suffer to redeem our loss.   Alleluia!

2 Hymns of praise then let us sing
Unto Christ, our heavenly King,
Who endured the cross and grave,
Sinners to redeem and save.   Alleluia!

3 But the pains which He endured,
Our salvation have procured;
Now above the sky He's King,
Where the angels ever sing.   Alleluia!

4 Sing we to our God above
Praise eternal as His love;
Praise Him all ye heavenly host,
Father, Son, and Holy Ghost;   Alleluia!
                                      Tate & Brady.

Easter.

JESUS, MEINE ZUVERSICHT. 7,8,7.
JOHANN CRÜGER.

Je-sus Christ, my sure de-fence, And my Sav-iour, ev-er liv-eth;

Know-ing this, my con-fi-dence Rests up-on the hope it giv-eth,

Tho' the night of death be fraught, Still with many an anx-ious thought. A-MEN.

113

2 Jesus, my Redeemer lives!
  I, too, unto life must waken;
He will have me where He is:
  Shall my courage then be shaken?
Shall I fear? Or could the Head
Rise and leave its members dead?

3 Nay, too closely am I bound
  Unto Him by hope for ever;
Faith's strong hand the Rock hath found,
  Grasped it, and will leave it never;
Not the bar of death can part
From its Lord the trusting heart.

4 What now sickens, mourns, and sighs,
  Christ with Him in glory bringeth;
Earthly is the seed and dies,
  Heavenly from the grave it springeth.
Natural is the death we die,
Spiritual our life on high.

5 Saviour, draw away our heart
  Now from pleasures base and hollow,
Let us there with Thee have part,
  Here on earth Thy foot-steps follow.
Fix our hearts beyond the skies,
Whither we ourselves would rise.

Louisa Hensel, of Frankenburg. Tr. Catherine Winkworth.

Easter.

CHRIST IS RISEN! 8,7. D.

FREDERICK C. MAKER.

Easter.

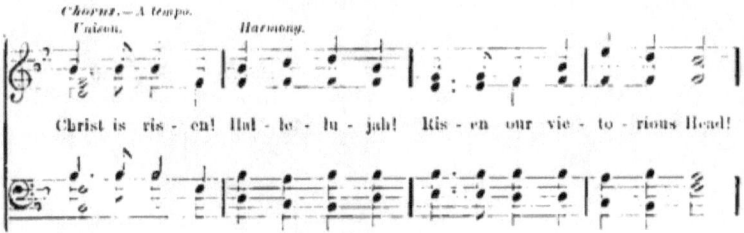

Christ is ris-en! Hal-le-lu-jah! Ris-en our vic-to-rious Head!

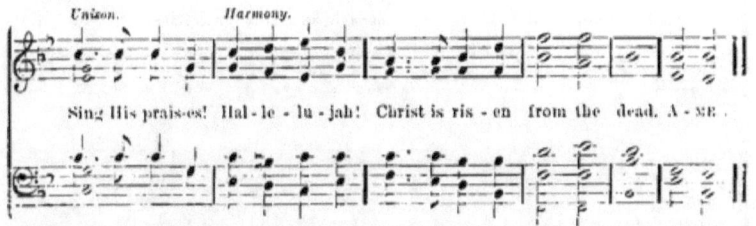

Sing His prais-es! Hal-le-lu-jah! Christ is ris-en from the dead. A-men.

114

2 Christ is risen! all the sadness
   Of our Lenten fast is o'er,
Through the open gates of gladness
   He returns to life once more:
Death and hell before Him bending,
   He doth rise, the Victor now,
Angels on His steps attending,
   Glory round His wounded brow:

    Cho.—Christ is risen! etc.

3 Christ is risen! all the sorrow
   That last evening round Him lay.
Now hath found a glorious morrow
   In the rising of to-day;
And the grave its first-fruits giveth,
   Springing up from holy ground,
He was dead, but now He liveth,
   He was lost, but He is found.

    Cho.—He is risen, etc.

4 Christ is risen! henceforth never
   Death or hell shall us enthrall,
But we Christ's, in Him for ever
   We have triumphed over all;
All the doubting and dejection
   Of our trembling hearts have ceased,
'Tis His day of Resurrection!
   Let us rise and keep the Feast:

    Cho.—Christ is risen! etc.

John S. B. Monsell.

Easter.

CHRIST IST ERSTANDEN. 7. With Hallelujah.

MICHAEL WEISS

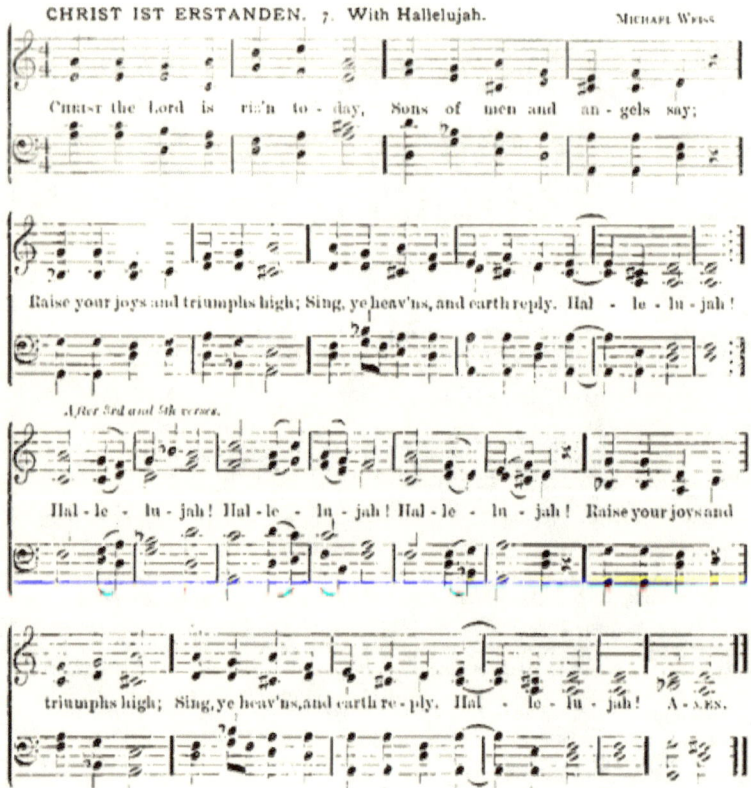

115

2 Vain the stone, the watch, the seal;
Christ has burst the gates of hell!
Death in vain forbids His rise;
Christ has opened Paradise.

3 Lives again our glorious King;
Where, O Death, is now Thy sting?
Dying once, He all doth save;
Where Thy victory, O Grave!

4 Soar we now where Christ has led,
Following our exalted Head;
Made like Him, like Him we rise;
Ours the cross, the grave, the skies!

5 Hail, the Lord of earth and heaven!
Praise to Thee by both be given:
Thee we greet triumphant now;
Hail, the resurrection Thou!

Charles Wesley.

Easter.

UNSER HERRSCHER, UNSER KÖNIG. 8,7,7. JOACHIM NEANDER.

He is ris-en, He is ris-en; Tell it out with joy-ful voice:
He has burst His three days' pris-on; Let the whole wide earth re-joice;
Death is conquered, man is free, Christ has won the vic-to-ry. A-MEN.

116

2 Come, ye sad and fearful-hearted,
   With glad smile and radiant brow:
Lent's long shadows have departed
   All His woes are over now,
And the passion that He bore:
Sin and pain can vex no more.

3 Come, with high and holy hymning,
   Chant our Lord's triumphant lay;
Not one darksome cloud is dimming
   Yonder glorious morning ray,
Breaking o'er the purple East,
Symbol of our Easter feast.

4 He is risen, He is risen;
   He hath opened heaven's gate:
We are free from sin's dark prison,
   Risen to a holier state;
And a brighter Easter beam
On our longing eyes shall stream.

                    Cecil F. Alexander.

117

2 God has still His angels, helping, at His word,
All His faithful children, like their faithful Lord;
Soothing them in sorrow, arming them in strife,
Opening wide the tomb-doors, leading into life.—*Cho.*

3 Father, send Thine angels unto us, we pray;
Leave us not to wander, all alone our way;
Let them guard and guide us, whereso'er we be,
Till our resurrection brings us home to Thee. *Cho.*

118

2 Our hearts be pure from evil,
  That we may see aright
The Lord in rays eternal
  Of resurrection-light;
And, listening to His accents,
  May hear so calm and plain
His own "All hail," and hearing,
  May raise the victor strain.

3 Now let the heavens be joyful,
  Let earth her song begin,
The round world keep high triumph,
  And all that is therein;
Let all things seen and unseen
  Their notes together blend,
For Christ the Lord is risen,
  Our joy that hath no end.

Tr. John M. Neale.

Ascension

ASCENSION. 7. With Hallelujah.　　　　　WILLIAM H. MONK.

Hail the day that sees Him rise, Hal - le - lu - jah!
Glo - rious to His na - tive skies! Hal - le - lu - jah!
Christ, a - while to mor - tals giv'n, Hal - le - lu - jah!
Re - as - cends His na - tive heav'n. Hal - le - lu - jah! A - men.

119

2 There for Him high triumph waits;
　Hallelujah!
Lift your heads, eternal gates!
　Hallelujah!
He hath conquerd death and sin,
　Hallelujah!
Take the King of Glory in.
　Hallelujah!

3 Lo, the heaven its Lord receives!
　Hallelujah!
Yet He loves the earth He leaves;
　Hallelujah!
Though returning to His throne,
　Hallelujah!
Still He calls mankind His own.
　Hallelujah!

　　　　　　　　Charles Wesley.

Ascension.

RUDOLSTADT. 7,6.
Justus H. Knecht.

O Christ, Thou hast ascended Triumphantly on high,
By cherub guards attended And armies of the sky. A-men.

120

2 There, there Thou standest pleading
   The virtue of Thy blood,
For sinners interceding,
   Our Advocate with God.

3 Heaven's gates unfold above Thee:
   But canst Thou, Lord, forget
The little band who love Thee
   And gaze from Olivet?

4 Oh, for the priceless merit
   Of Thy redeeming cross,
Vouchsafe Thy sevenfold Spirit,
   And turn to gain our loss;

5 Till we by strong endeavor
   In heart and mind ascend,
And dwell with Thee for ever
   In raptures without end.
                        Edward H. Bickersteth.

121

Draw us to Thee, Lord Jesus,
   And we will hasten on;
For strong desire doth seize us
   To go where Thou art gone.

2 Draw us to Thee; enlighten
   These hearts to find Thy way,
That else the tempests frighten,
   Or pleasures lure astray.

3 Draw us to Thee; and teach us
   E'en now that rest to find,
Where turmoils cannot reach us,
   Nor cares weigh down the mind.

4 Draw us to Thee; nor leave us
   Till all our path is trod,
Then in Thine arms receive us,
   And bear us home to God.
         Ludaemilia Elizabeth. Tr. Catherine Winkworth.

Whitsuntide

ST. OSWALD. L. M.
John B. Dykes.

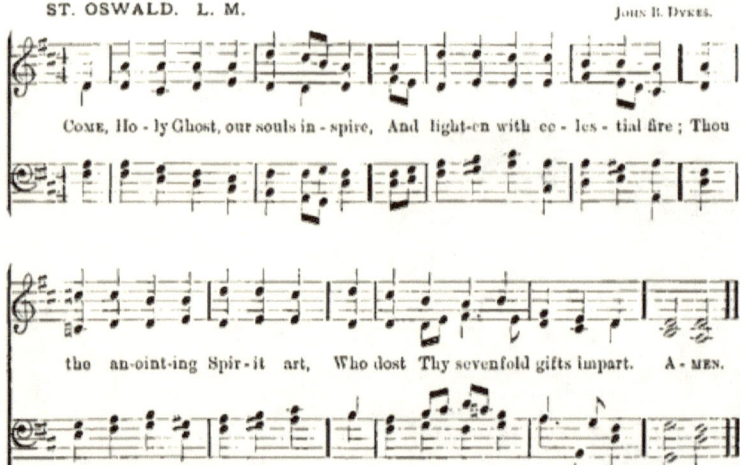

Come, Ho-ly Ghost, our souls in-spire, And light-en with ce-les-tial fire; Thou the an-oint-ing Spir-it art, Who dost Thy sevenfold gifts impart. A-MEN.

122

2 Thy blessed unction from above,
Is comfort, life, and fire of love,
Enable with perpetual light
The dullness of our blinded sight.

3 Anoint our heart and cheer our face
With the abundance of Thy grace.

Keep far our foes; give peace at home:
Where Thou art Guide, no ill can come.

4 Teach us to know the Father, Son,
And Thee of Both, to be but One;
That through the ages all along,
Thy praise may be our endless song!

Tr. John Cosin.

KOMM, HEILIGER GEIST. L. M. D. With Hallelujah.
1524.

Come, Ho-ly Spir-it, God and Lord! Be all Thy grac-es now out-pour'd

Whitsuntide.

On the be-liev-er's mind and soul, To strengthen, save, and make us whole. Lord, by the brightness of Thy light, Thou in the faith dost men u-nite Of ev-ery land and ev-ery tongue: This to Thy praise, O Lord, O Lord, be sung. Hal-le-lu — jah, Hal-le-lu — jah. A-MEN.

123

2 Thou strong Defence, Thou holy Light,
Teach us to know our God aright,
And call Him Father from the heart:
The Word of life and truth impart:
That we may love not doctrines strange,
Nor e'er to other teachers range,
But Jesus for our Master own,
And put our trust in Him, in Him alone.

3 Thou sacred Ardor, Comfort sweet,
Help us to wait with ready feet
And willing heart at Thy command,
Nor trial fright us from Thy band.
Lord, make us ready with Thy powers;
Strengthen the flesh in weaker hours,
That as good warriors we may force
Through life and death to Thee, to Thee our
course! Martin Luther. Tr. Catherine Winkworth.

Whitsuntide

MERCY. 7.   LOUIS M. GOTTSCHALK.

Holy Ghost! with light divine, Shine upon this heart of mine; Chase the shades of night away, Turn my darkness into day. A-MEN.

Used by arr. with O. Ditson Co., owners of copyright.

124
Holy Ghost! with light divine,
Shine upon this heart of mine;
Chase the shades of night away,
Turn my darkness into day.

2 Holy Ghost! with power divine,
Cleanse this guilty heart of mine;
Long hath sin, without control,
Held dominion o'er my soul.

3 Holy Ghost! with joy divine,
Cheer this saddened heart of mine;
Bid my many woes depart,
Heal my wounded, bleeding heart.

4 Holy Spirit! all divine,
Dwell within this heart of mine
Cast down every idol-throne,
Reign supreme — and reign alone.
Andrew Reed.

125
Gracious Spirit, Love divine!
Let Thy light within me shine;
All my guilty fears remove,
Fill me with Thy heavenly love.

2 Speak Thy pardoning grace to me,
Set the burdened sinner free;
Lead me to the Lamb of God;
Wash me in His precious blood.

3 Life and peace to me impart,
Seal salvation on my heart;
Breathe Thyself into my breast, —
Earnest of immortal rest.

4 Let me never from Thee stray,
Keep me in the narrow way;
Fill my soul with joy divine,
Keep me, Lord! for ever Thine.
John Stocker.

Whitsuntide.

KOMM, O KOMM DU GEIST DES LEBENS. 8.7.7.

Come, O come, Thou quick'ning Spir-it, Thou for ev-er art di-vine;
Let Thy pow-er nev-er fail me, Al-ways fill this heart of mine;
Thus shall grace, and truth, and light Dis-si-pate the gloom of night. A-men.

126

2 Grant my mind and my affections
  Wisdom, counsel, purity,
That I may be ever seeking
  Naught but that which pleases Thee.
Let Thy knowledge spread and grow,
Working error's overthrow.

3 Lead me to green pastures, lead me
  By the true and living way;
Shield me from each strong temptation
  That might draw my heart astray;
And if e'er my feet should turn,
For each error let me mourn.

4 In the faith O make me steadfast;
  Let not Satan, death or shame
Of my confidence deprive me;
  Lord, my refuge is Thy name.
When the flesh inclines to ill,
Let Thy Word prove stronger still.

5 And when my last hour approaches,
  Let my hopes grow yet more bright
(Since I am an heir of heaven),
  In Thy glorious courts of light,
Fairer far than voice can tell,
There redeemed by Christ to dwell.

Heinrich Held. Tr. Charles W. Schaeffer.

Whitsuntide.

O HEIL'GER GEIST. P. M.
Philipp Nicolai.

O Holy Spirit, enter in, Among these hearts Thy work begin,
Sun of the soul, Thou Light Divine, Around and in us brightly shine.
Thy temple deign to make us;
To strength and gladness wake us,
Where Thou shinest, Life from heaven There is given. We before Thee For that precious gift implore Thee. A-MEN.

127

2 Left to ourselves we shall but stray;
O lead us on the narrow way,
  With wisest counsel guide us,
And give us steadfastness, that we
May henceforth truly follow Thee,
  Whatever woes betide us:
Heal Thou gently, Hearts now broken,
    Give some token
      Thou art near us,
Whom we trust to light and cheer us.

3 O mighty Rock! O Source of Life,
Let Thy dear Word, 'mid doubt and strife,
  Be so within us burning,
That we be faithful unto death,
In Thy pure love and holy faith,
  From Thee true wisdom learning!
Lord, Thy graces, On us shower,
    By Thy power
      Christ confessing,
Let us win His grace and blessing.

4 Grant that our days, while life shall last,
In purest holiness be past;
  Our minds so rule and strengthen
That they may rise o'er things of earth,
The hopes and joys that here have birth;
  And if our course Thou lengthen,
Keep Thou pure, Lord, From offences,
    Heart and senses;
      Blessed Spirit,
Bid us thus true life inherit.

Michael Schirmer. *Tr.* Catherine Winkworth.

Whitsuntide.

DOVER. S. M.   Aaron Williams' Coll.

Lord God, the Ho-ly Ghost! In this ac-cept-ed hour, As on the day of Pen-te-cost, De-scend in all Thy pow'r. A-men.

128

2 We meet with one accord
   In our appointed place,
And wait the promise of our Lord,
   The Spirit of all grace.

3 Like mighty rushing wind
   Upon the waves beneath,
Move with one impulse every mind
   One soul, one feeling breathe.

4 Spirit of Light, explore,
   And chase our gloom away;
With lustre shining more and more,
   Unto the perfect day!

5 Spirit of Truth, be Thou
   In life and death our Guide;
O Spirit of adoption, now
   May we be sanctified!

James Montgomery.

129

Come, Holy Spirit, come;
   Let Thy bright beams arise;
Dispel the sorrow from our minds,
   The darkness from our eyes.

2 Revive our drooping faith,
   Our doubts and fears remove,
And kindle in our breasts the flame
   Of never-dying love.

3 Convince us of our sin;
   Then lead to Jesus' blood,
And to our wondering view reveal
   The mercies of our God.

4 'Tis Thine to cleanse the heart,
   To sanctify the soul,
To pour fresh life in every part,
   And new-create the whole.

Joseph Hart. Alt. by Augustus M. Toplady.

Whitsuntide.

CHENIES. 7,6. D. — Timothy R. Matthews

O enter, Lord, Thy temple, Be Thou my spirit's Guest,
Who at my birth didst give me A second birth more blest.
Though here to dwell Thou deignest, Thou in the Godhead, Lord,
For ever equal reignest, Art equally adored. A-MEN.

130

2 O enter, let me know Thee,
  And feel Thy power within,
The power that breaks our fetters,
  And rescues us from sin.
That I may serve Thee truly,
  O wash and cleanse Thou me,
To render honor duly
  With perfect heart to Thee.

3 Order our path in all things
  According to Thy mind,
And when this life is over,
  And all must be resigned,
With calm and fearless spirit
  O grant us then to die,
And after death inherit
  Eternal life on high.

Paul Gerhardt. Tr. Catherine Winkworth.

131

2 Thou, of all consolers best,
Visiting the troubled breast,
  Dost refreshing peace bestow;
Thou in toil art comfort sweet,
Pleasant coolness in the heat,
  Solace in the midst of woe.

3 Light immortal! Light divine!
Visit Thou these hearts of Thine,
  And our inmost being fill:
If Thou take Thy grace away,
Nothing pure in man will stay;
  All his good is turned to ill.

4 Heal our wounds, our strength renew;
On our dryness pour Thy dew;
  Wash the stains of guilt away:
Bend the stubborn heart and will;
Melt the frozen, warm the chill;
  Guide the steps that go astray.

5 Thou, on those who evermore
Thee confess and Thee adore,
  In Thy sevenfold gifts, descend;
Give them comfort when they die,
Give them life with Thee on high,
  Give them joys which never end.

Tr. Edward Caswall.

New Year.

CYPRUS. 7. Ad. fr. Felix Mendelssohn-Bartholdy.

For Thy mer-cy and Thy grace, Faith-ful through an-oth-er year,

Hear our song of thank-ful-ness; Je-sus, our Re-deem-er, hear. A-MEN.

132

2 In our weakness and distress,
   Rock of strength, be Thou our stay;
In the pathless wilderness
   Be our true and living way.

3 Who of us death's awful road
   In the coming year shall tread,
With Thy rod and staff, O God,
   Comfort Thou his dying bed.

4 Keep us faithful, keep us pure,
   Keep us evermore Thine own,
Help, oh, help us to endure;
   Fit us for the promised crown.

5 So within Thy palace gate
   We shall praise, on golden strings,
Thee the only Potentate,
   Lord of lords and King of kings.
                              Henry Downton.

133

WHILE, with ceaseless course, the sun
   Hasted through the former year,
Many souls their race have run,
   Never more to meet us here:

2 Fixed in an eternal state,
   They have done with all below;
We a little longer wait,
   But how little—none can know.

3 Thanks for mercies past receive;
   Pardon of our sins renew;
Teach us henceforth how to live
   With eternity in view:

4 Bless Thy word to young and old;
   Fill us with a Saviour's love;
And when life's short tale is told,
   May we dwell with Him above.
                              John Newton.

The Old Year.

ST. MARKS. S. M. D.
George C. F. Haas.

A few more years shall roll, A few more seasons come, And we shall be with those that rest A-sleep with-in the tomb; Then, O my Lord, pre-pare My soul for that great day; Oh, wash me in Thy precious blood, And take my sins a-way. A-MEN.

Copyright, 1895. Rev. George C. F. Haas.

134

2 A few more struggles here,
A few more partings o'er,
A few more toils, a few more tears,
And we shall weep no more;
Then, O my Lord, prepare
My soul for that bright day;
Oh, wash me in Thy precious blood,
And take my sins away.

3 'Tis but a little while
And He shall come again,
Who died that we might live, Who lives
That we with Him may reign:
Then, O my Lord, prepare
My soul for that glad day;
Oh, wash me in Thy precious blood,
And take my sins away.

Horatius Bonar.

100 Festival.

LUTHER LEAGUE RALLY HYMN. 7,6,5.
GEORGE C. F. HAAS.

Oh, Christians! leagued to-geth-er, To bat-tle for the right, A-rise, and don your ar-mor, Put the foe to flight; We've giv-en our al-le-giance To serve without sur-cease, The might-y Lord of Ar-mies And gen-tle Prince of Peace.

Chorus.

All hail, our Roy-al Col-ors, For King-ly lives un-fold, Be-neath our Lu-ther En-sign, Black, red, white blue and gold. A-MEN.

Copyright, 1897, by the LUTHER LEAGUE REVIEW.

Festivals.

135

2 Then onward be the war-cry
  And onward still, so long
As we have self to conquer,
  Souls to cheer with song.
Let sound the martial music,
  Ring out the bugle call
To rally for the conflict
  Our people one and all!—*Cho.*

3 We proudly bear as banner
  A cross within the heart
To show that we have chosen
  Christ, the better part.
Then joy and peace and comfort
  Shall blossom as a rose
Until our earthly blessings
  The worth of Heaven disclose. —*Cho.*
                    Mrs. Lillian W. Cassedy.

AMERICA. 6,4.   Henry Carey, arr.

My coun-try 'tis of thee, Sweet land of lib-er-ty, Of thee I sing:
Land where my fa-thers died! Land of the Pil-grims' pride! From ev-ery
mountain side Let freedom ring! A-men.

136

2 My native country, thee—
  Land of the noble, free—
    Thy name I love;
  I love thy rocks and rills,
  Thy woods and templed hills;
  My heart with rapture thrills
    Like that above

3 Let music swell the breeze,
  And ring from all the trees
    Sweet freedom's song;
  Let mortal tongues awake;
  Let all that breathe partake;
  Let rocks their silence break,—
    The sound prolong.

4 Our fathers' God! to Thee,
  Author of liberty,
    To Thee we sing:
  Long may our land be bright
  With freedom's holy light;
  Protect us by Thy might,
    Great God, our King!
              Samuel F. Smith.

137

2 Lord of the harvest, all is Thine:
The rains that fall, the suns that shine,
The seed once hidden in the ground,
The skill that makes our fruits abound:
New every year Thy gifts appear;
New praises from our lips shall sound.

3 But chiefly when Thy liberal hand
Bestows new plenty o'er the land,
When sounds of music fill the air,
As homeward all their treasures bear:
Then will we raise our hymn of praise,
For we Thy common bounties share.

4 Immortal honor, endless fame
Attend th'Almighty Father's name;
Like honor to th' Incarnate Son,
Who for lost man redemption won;
And equal praise we thankful raise
To Thee, Blest Spirit, with them One.

John H. Gurney.

Harvest.

ST. GEORGE'S. 7. D. George J. Elvey.

Come, ye thankful people, come, Raise the song of Harvest Home! All is safe-ly gathered in, Ere the win-ter storms be-gin: God our Mak-er doth pro-vide For our wants to be supplied; Come to God's own temple, come, Raise the song of Harvest Home! AMEN.

138

2 We ourselves are God's own field,
Fruit unto His praise to yield:
Wheat and tares together sown,
Unto joy or sorrow grown:
First the blade, and then the ear,
Then the full corn shall appear:
Grant, O Harvest-Lord, that we
Wholesome grain and pure may be!

3 For the Lord our God shall come,
And shall take His harvest home;
From His field shall in that day
All offences purge away:

Give His angels charge at last
In the fire the tares to cast:
But the fruitful ears to store
In His garner evermore.

4 Then, thou Church Triumphant, come,
Raise the song of Harvest Home!
All are safely gathered in,
Free from sorrow, free from sin-
There, for ever purified,
In God's garner to abide:
Come, ten thousand angels, come,
Raise the glorious Harvest Home!

Henry Alford.

139

2 He only is the maker
   Of all things near and far;
He paints the wayside flowers,
   He lights the ev'ning star;
The winds and waves obey Him,
   By Him the birds are fed;
Much more to us, His children,
   He gives our daily bread.—*Cho.*

3 We thank Thee, then, O Father,
   For all things bright and good;
The seed-time and the harvest,
   Our life, our health, our food;
Accept the gifts we offer,
   For all Thy love imparts,
And, what Thou most desirest,
   Our humble, thankful hearts.—*Cho.*

Tr. Jane M. Campbell.

Festival of the Reformation.

EIN' FESTE BURG IST UNSER GOTT. 8,7,5,6,7.   Martin Luther.

A might-y For-tress is our God, A trust-y Shield and Wea-pon;
He helps us free from ev-'ry need That hath us now o'er-tak-en.
The old bit-ter foe Means us dead-ly woe; Deep guile and great might
Are his dread arms in fight, On earth is not his e-qual. A-men.

140

2 With might of ours can naught be done,
  Soon were our loss effected;
But for us fights the Valiant One
  Whom God Himself elected.
    Ask ye, Who is this?
    Jesus Christ it is,
  Of Sabaoth Lord,
  And there's none other God,
He holds the field for ever.

3 Though devils all the world should fill,
  All watching to devour us,
We tremble not, we fear no ill,
  They cannot overpower us.
    This world's prince may still
    Scowl fierce as he will,
  He can harm us none,
  He's judged, the deed is done,
One little word o'erthrows him.

4 The Word they still shall let remain,
  And not a thank have for it,
He's by our side upon the plain,
  With His good gifts and Spirit.
    Take they then our life,
    Goods, fame, child, and wife;
  When their worst is done,
  They yet have nothing won,
The Kingdom ours remaineth.

Martin Luther.

Festival of the Reformation.

ELLACOMBE. C. M. D.

Lord, not to us,—we claim it not,—To Thee be all the praise,
That no profane and sinful spot Our mother Church o'erlays;
That, as in her primeval days, From intermediate stain
Cleans'd by Thy Word, to Thee she pays Unsullied rites again. A-MEN.

141

2 To no material form confined,
   A Spirit pure alone,
We serve Thee not in likeness shrined
   Of bread, or wood, or stone:
Nor saint nor angel at Thy throne
   We crave to intercede;
With Thee, for our misdeeds atone,
   With Thee, for mercy plead.

3 But far remote we seek Thy face,
   Hid in Thy heavenly seat:
And, sole Transmitter of Thy grace,
   The Saviour's name entreat:
And thus to Thee with honor meet
   We hymn the grateful lay,
Whose Word recalled our erring feet,
   And taught us how to pray.

                Richard Mant.

Festival of the Reformation.

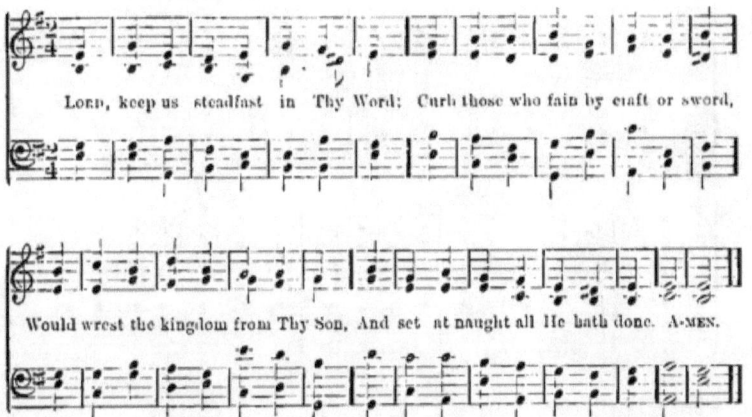

142

2 Lord Jesus Christ, Thy power make known;
For Thou art Lord of lords alone:
Defend Thy Christendom, that we
May evermore sing praise to Thee.

3 O Comforter, of priceless worth,
Send peace and unity on earth,
Support us in our final strife,
And lead us out of death to life.
Martin Luther. *Tr.* Catherine Winkworth.

143

Lord Jesus Christ, with us abide,
While fall the shades of eventide;
Let not the radiant light divine
Of Thy dear word e'er cease to shine.

2 In these sad latter days may we,
Vouchsafe this, Lord, e'er steadfast be,
And keep Thy word and sacrament
In purity unto the end.

3 Rebuke the spirits that, in pride
Exalting self, would set aside
Thy word, and bring devices new,
Corrupting, Lord, Thy doctrine true.

4 Not ours the cause is, but Thine own;
Not ours the glory, Thine alone;
Wherefore Thy people, Lord, defend,
Who trustingly in Thee depend.

5 Our heart's firm trust is e'er Thy word,
It is Thy Church's shield, and sword:
O, keep us fast in this, we pray,
That we may seek no other way.

6 Grant that according to Thy word
We here may live, and dying, Lord,
Still trusting in Thy word may we
Leave earth's sad vale to be with Thee.
N Selnecker. *Tr.* George C. F. Haas.

108 Processional.

VICTORY. P. M.   Joseph Barnby.

Processional.

144

2 Our sword is the Spirit of God on high,
  Our helmet is His salvation,
Our banner, the Cross of Calvary,
  Our watchword, the Incarnation.
    We march, we march, etc.

3 And the choir of angels with song awaits
  Our march to the golden Sion;
For our Captain has broken the brazen gates,
  And burst the bars of iron.
    We march, we march, etc.

4 Then onward we march, our arms to prove,
  With the banner of Christ before us,
With His eye of love looking down from above,
  And His holy arm spread o'er us.
    We march, we march, etc.

Gerard Moultrie.

110 Processional.

MARION. S. M. With Chorus.　　　　　　　　　Arthur H. Messiter.

Re - joice, ye pure in heart! Re - joice, give thanks, and sing!

Your glo - rious ban - ner wave on high, The cross of Christ your King!

Chorus.

Re - joice,　　re - joice,　　re - joice, give thanks and sing. A - men.

re - joice,　re - joice,

Used by permission.

145

2 With all the angel choirs,
  With all the saints of earth,
Pour out the strains of joy and bliss,
  True rapture, noblest mirth!—*Cho.*

3 Your clear hosannas raise,
  And alleluias loud!
Whilst answering echoes upward float,
  Like wreaths of incense cloud.—*Cho.*

4 Yes, on through life's long path!
  Still chanting as ye go;
From youth to age, by night and day,
  In gladness and in woe.—*Cho.*

5 Still lift your standard high!
  Still march in firm array!
As warriors through the darkness toil,
  Till dawns the golden day!—*Cho.*

6 At last the march shall end;
  The wearied ones shall rest;
The pilgrims find their Father's house,
  Jerusalem the blest.—*Cho.*

7 Then on, ye pure in heart!
  Rejoice, give thanks, and sing!
Your glorious banner wave on high,
  The cross of Christ your King!—*Cho.*
  　　　　　　　　Edward H. Plumptre.

Processional.

WATCHWORD. 6,5, 12 lines.   JAMES C. KNOX

Forward! be our watchword, Steps and voices joined; Seek the things before us,
Not a look behind: Burns the fi-ery pil-lar At our ar-my's head;
Who shall dream of shrinking, By our Cap-tain led? Forward thro' the des-ert,
Thro' the toil and fight! Jor-dan flows be-fore us; Si-on beams with light. A-MEN.

146
2 Glories upon glories
  Hath our God prepared,
By the souls that love Him
  One day to be shared;
Eye hath not beheld them,
  Ear hath never heard;
Nor of these hath uttered
  Thought or speech a word;
Forward! marching eastward
  Where the heaven is bright,
Till the veil be lifted,
  Till our faith be sight.

3 To th' eternal Father
  Loudest anthems raise.
To the Son and Spirit
  Echo songs of praise:
To the Lord of glory,
  Blessèd Three in One,
Be by men and angels
  Endless honor done.
Weak are earthly praises,
  Dull the songs of night:
Forward into triumph!
  Forward into light!   Henry Alford.

147

2 Nearer, ever nearer,
  Christ, we draw to Thee,
Deep in adoration
  Bending low the knee:
Thou for our redemption
  Cam'st on earth to die:
Thou, that we might follow,
  Hast gone up on high.

3 Great, and ever greater
  Are Thy mercies here,
True and everlasting
  Are the glories there;
Where no pain, or sorrow,
  Toil or care, is known,
Where the angel legions
  Circle round Thy throne.

4 Clearer still, and clearer,
  Dawns the light from heaven,
In our sadness bringing
  News of sins forgiven;
Life has lost its shadows;
  Pure the light within;
Thou hast shed Thy radiance
  On a world of sin.

5 Brighter still, and brighter,
  Glows the western sun,
Shedding all its gladness
  O'er our work that's done;
Time will soon be over,
  Toil and sorrow past,
May we, blessèd Saviour,
  Find a rest at last!

Godfrey Thring.

Processional.

ST. DAVID. 6,5. D. John B. Calkin.

At the name of Jesus Every knee shall bow, Every tongue confess Him King of glory now; 'Tis the Father's pleasure We should call Him Lord, Who from the beginning Was the mighty Word. A-men.

148

2 Humbled for a season,
  To receive a Name
From the lips of sinners,
  Unto whom He came,
Faithfully He bore it
  Spotless to the last,
Brought it back victorious,
  When from death He passed;

3 Bore it up triumphant,
  With its human light,
Through all ranks of creatures,
  To the central height;
To the throne of Godhead,
  To the Father's breast,
Filled it with the glory
  Of that perfect rest.

4 In your hearts enthrone Him;
  There let Him subdue
All that is not holy,
  All that is not true:
Crown Him as your Captain
  In temptation's hour;
Let His will enfold you
  In its light and power.

5 Brothers, this Lord Jesus
  Shall return again,
With His Father's glory,
  With His angel train;
For all wreaths of empire
  Meet upon His brow,
And our hearts confess Him
  King of glory now.

Caroline M. Noel.

Our Faith.

THACHER. S. M. — GEORGE F. HANDEL.

The Lord my Shepherd is; I shall be well sup-plied: Since He is mine, and I am His What can I want be-side? A-MEN.

149

2 He leads me to the place
  Where heavenly pasture grows;
Where living waters gently pass,
  And full salvation flows.

3 While He affords His aid,
  I cannot yield to fear:
Tho' I should walk thro' death's dark shade,
  My Shepherd's with me there.

4 In spite of all my foes,
  Thou dost my table spread;
My cup with blessings overflows,
  And joy exalts my head.

5 The bounties of Thy love
  Shall crown my following days;
Nor from Thy house will I remove,
  Nor cease to speak Thy praise.
              Isaac Watts.

150

"My times are in Thy hand;"
  My God, I wish them there;
My life, my friends, my soul, I leave
  Entirely to Thy care.

2 "My times are in Thy hand;"
  Why should I doubt or fear?
My Father's hand will never cause
  His child a needless tear.

3 "My times are in Thy hand,"
  Jesus, the Crucified!
The hand my cruel sins had pierced
  Is now my Guard and Guide.

4 "My times are in Thy hand;"
  I'll always trust in Thee;
And, after death, at Thy right hand
  I shall forever be.
              William F. Lloyd.

Our Faith.   115

ST. STEPHEN'S. C. M.   WILLIAM JONES.

God moves in a mys-te-rious way, His won-ders to per-form:
He plants His foot-steps in the sea, And rides up-on the storm. A-MEN.

151

2 Deep in unfathomable mines
   Of never-failing skill,
He treasures up His bright designs,
   And works His sovereign will.

3 Ye fearful saints, fresh courage take:
   The clouds ye so much dread
Are big with mercy, and shall break
   In blessings on your head.

4 Judge not the Lord by feeble sense,
   But trust Him for His grace;
Behind a frowning Providence
   He hides a smiling face.

5 Blind unbelief is sure to err,
   And scan His works in vain;
God is His own interpreter,
   And He will make it plain.
               William Cowper.

152

O God of Jacob, by whose hand
   Thy people still are fed;
Who, through this weary pilgrimage
   Hast all our fathers led!

2 To Thee our humble vows we raise,
   To Thee address our prayer;
And in Thy kind and faithful breast
   Deposit all our care.

3 Through each perplexing path of life
   Our wandering footsteps guide;
Give us each day our daily bread,
   And raiment fit provide.

4 O spread Thy covering wings around,
   Till all our wanderings cease;
And at our Father's loved abode
   Our souls arrive in peace.
               Philip Doddridge.

153

2 I heard the voice of Jesus say,
  "Behold, I freely give
The living water; thirsty one,
  Stoop down, and drink, and live."
I came to Jesus and I drank
  Of that life-giving stream;
My thirst was quenched, my soul revived,
  And now I live in Him.

3 I heard the voice of Jesus say,
  "I am this dark world's Light;
Look unto me, thy morn shall rise,
  And all thy day be bright."
I looked to Jesus, and I found
  In Him, my Star, my Sun;
And in that Light of life I'll walk,
  Till travelling days are done.

Horatius Bonar.

Our Faith.

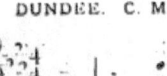

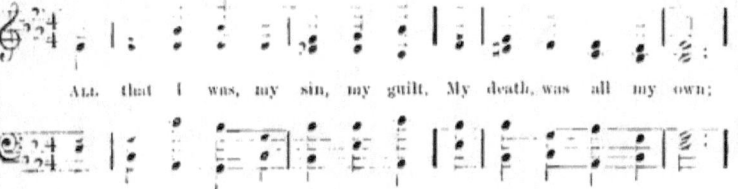

All that I was, my sin, my guilt, My death, was all my own;

All that I am, I owe to Thee, My gracious God, alone. A-men.

154

2 The evil of my former state
  Was mine, and only mine;
The good in which I now rejoice
  Is Thine, and only Thine.

3 The darkness of my former state,
  The bondage, all was mine;
The light of life in which I walk,
  The liberty, is Thine.

4 Thy grace first made me feel my sin,
  It taught me to believe;
Then in believing, peace I found,
  And now I live, I live.

5 All that I am, e'en here on earth,
  All that I hope to be
When Jesus comes and glory dawns,
  I owe it, Lord, to Thee.

Horatius Bonar.

155

SHINE on our souls, eternal God!
  With rays of beauty shine;
O let Thy favor crown our days,
  And all their round be Thine.

2 Did we not raise our hands to Thee,
  Our hands might toil in vain;
Small joy success itself could give,
  If Thou Thy love restrain.

3 With Thee let every week begin,
  With Thee each day be spent,
For Thee each fleeting hour improved,
  Since each by Thee is lent.

4 Thus cheer us through this toilsome road,
  Till all our labors cease;
And heaven refresh our weary souls
  With everlasting peace.

Philip Doddridge.

Our Faith.

156

2 Other refuge have I none;
 Hangs my helpless soul on Thee;
Leave, ah! leave me not alone,
 Still support and comfort me.
All my trust on Thee is stayed;
 All my help from Thee I bring;
Cover my defenceless head
 With the shadow of Thy wing.

3 Thou, O Christ! art all I want;
 More than all in Thee I find;
Raise the fallen, cheer the faint,
 Heal the sick, and lead the blind.
Just and holy is Thy name,
 I am all unrighteousness;
Vile and full of sin I am,
 Thou art full of truth and grace.

4 Plenteous grace with Thee is found,—
 Grace to pardon all my sin;
Let the healing streams abound,
 Make and keep me pure within;
Thou of life the Fountain art,
 Freely let me take of Thee;
Spring Thou up within my heart,
 Rise to all eternity.

Charles Wesley.

Our Faith.

WHITTINGHAM. 6. John S. B. Hodges.

Thy life was given for me! Thy blood, O Lord, was shed;
That I might ransom'd be,...... And quicken'd from the dead.
Thy life was given for me: What have I given for Thee? A-MEN.

Used by permission.

157

2 Long years were spent for me
In weariness and woe,
That through eternity
Thy glory I might know.
   Long years were spent for me:
   Have I spent one for Thee?

3 Thy Father's home of light,
Thy rainbow-circled throne,
Were left for earthly night,
For wanderings sad and lone.
   Yea, all was left for me:
   Have I left aught for Thee?

4 And Thou hast brought to me,
Down from Thy home above,
Salvation full and free,
Thy pardon and Thy love.
   Great gifts Thou broughtest me:
   What have I brought to Thee?

5 Oh, let my life be given,
My years for Thee be spent!
World fetters all be riven,
And joy with suffering blent!
   Thou gavest Thyself for me:
   I give myself to Thee.

Frances R. Havergal.

Our Faith.

STOWELL. L. M.  Solon Wilder.

158

2 There is a place, where Jesus sheds
The oil of gladness on our heads,—
A place, than all besides, more sweet;
It is the blood-bought mercy-seat.

3 There is a scene where spirits blend,
Where friend holds fellowship with friend;
Though sundered far, by faith they meet
Around one common mercy-seat.

4 There, there, on eagle wings we soar,
And sin and sense molest no more,
And heaven comes down our souls to greet,
And glory crowns the mercy-seat!

5 Oh, let my hand forget her skill,
My tongue be silent, cold, and still,
This bounding heart forget to beat,
If I forget the mercy-seat!

Hugh Stowell.

Our Faith.

HESPERUS. L. M.   Henry Baker.

Just as I am, without one plea, But that Thy blood was shed for me,

And that Thou bid'st me come to Thee, O Lamb of God, I come, I come. A-MEN.

159

2 Just as I am, and waiting not
To rid my soul of one dark blot,
To Thee, whose Blood can cleanse each spot,
O Lamb of God, I come, I come!

3 Just as I am, though tossed about
With many a conflict, many a doubt,
Fightings and fears within, without,
O Lamb of God, I come, I come!

4 Just as I am; Thou wilt receive,
Wilt welcome, pardon, cleanse, relieve,
Because Thy promise I believe;
O Lamb of God, I come, I come!

5 Just as I am; Thy Love unknown
Has broken every barrier down;
Now to be Thine, yea, Thine alone,
O Lamb of God, I come, I come!
          Charlotte Elliott.

160

I THIRST, Thou wounded Lamb of God,
To wash me in Thy cleansing Blood;
To dwell within Thy wounds; then pain
Is sweet, and life or death is gain.

2 Take my poor heart, and let it be
For ever closed to all but Thee!
Seal Thou my breast, and let me wear
That pledge of love for ever there.

3 What are our works but sin and death,
Till Thou Thy quickening Spirit breathe?
Thou giv'st the power Thy grace to move;
O wondrous grace! O boundless Love!

4 Ah Lord, enlarge our scanty thought,
To know the wonders Thou hast wrought;
Unloose our stammering tongues, to tell
Thy Love immense, unsearchable!
        Tr. John Wesley.

Our Faith.

TOPLADY. 7, 6 lines. THOMAS HASTINGS.

161

Rock of Ages, cleft for me!
Let me hide myself in Thee;
Let the water and the blood,
From Thy wounded side that flowed,
Be of sin the perfect cure;
Save me, Lord! and make me pure.

2 Not the labors of my hands
Can fulfil Thy law's demands;
Could my zeal no languor know,
Could my tears for ever flow,
All for sin could not atone,
Thou must save and Thou alone:

3 Nothing in my hand I bring;
Simply to Thy cross I cling.
Naked, come to Thee for dress,
Helpless, look to Thee for grace;
Foul, I to the fountain fly
Wash me, Saviour, or I die.

4 While I draw this fleeting breath,
When my eye-lids close in death,
When I rise to worlds unknown,
And behold Thee on Thy throne,
Rock of Ages, cleft for me!
Let me hide myself in Thee.

Augustus M. Toplady.

Our Faith

ALMA. 11,10. SAMUEL WEBBE.

Come, ye dis-con-so-late, wher-e'er ye lan-guish, Come to the mer-cy-seat, fer-vent-ly kneel, Here bring your wounded hearts, here tell your an-guish; Earth hath no sor-row that heav'n can-not heal. A-MEN.

162

Come, ye disconsolate, where'er ye languish,
  Come to the mercy-seat, fervently kneel,
Here bring your wounded hearts, here tell your anguish;
  Earth hath no sorrow that heaven cannot heal.

2 Joy of the comfortless, light of the straying,
  Hope of the penitent, fadeless and pure;
Here speaks the Comforter, tenderly saying—
  Earth hath no sorrow that heaven cannot cure.

3 Here see the Bread of life; see waters flowing
  Forth from the throne of God, pure from above;
Come to the feast of love; come, ever knowing
  Earth hath no sorrow but heaven can remove.

Ver. 1 and 2—Thomas Moore. Ver. 3—Thomas Hastings.

Our Faith.

SPANISH HYMN. 7, 6 lines.

Je-sus, Mas-ter, whose I am, Purchased Thine a-lone to be,
By Thy blood, O spot-less Lamb, Shed so will-ing-ly for me;
Let my heart be all Thine own, Let me live to Thee a-lone. A-MEN.

163

2 Other lords have long held sway;
  Now Thy name alone to bear,
Thy dear voice alone obey,
  Is my daily, hourly prayer.
Whom have I in heaven but Thee?
Nothing else my joy can be.

3 Jesus, Master, I am Thine;
  Keep me faithful, keep me near;
Let Thy presence in me shine
  All my homeward way to cheer.
Jesus, at Thy feet I fall,
Oh, be Thou my All in all.
Frances R. Havergal.

164

BLESSED Saviour! Thee I love,
  All my other joys above;
All my hopes in Thee abide,
  Thou my hope, and naught beside:
Ever let my glory be,
Only, only, only Thee.

2 Blessed Saviour, Thine am I,
  Thine to live and Thine to die;
Height, or depth, or earthly power,
  Ne'er shall hide my Saviour more:
Ever shall my glory be
Only, only, only Thee.
George Duffield.

Our Faith.

ERFURTH. 8,5,3.   Hubert P. Main.

165

2 Precious blood, that hath redeemed us!
    All the price is paid;
Perfect pardon now is offered,
    Peace is made.

3 Though thy sins are red like crimson,
    Deep in scarlet glow,
Jesus' precious blood shall wash thee
    White as snow.

4 Precious blood! by this we conquer
    In the fiercest fight,
Sin and Satan overcoming
    By its might.

5 Precious, precious blood of Jesus,
    Ever flowing free!
O believe it, O receive it,
    'Tis for Thee!

Frances R. Havergal.

BULLINGER. 8,5,3.   Ethelbert W. Bullinger.

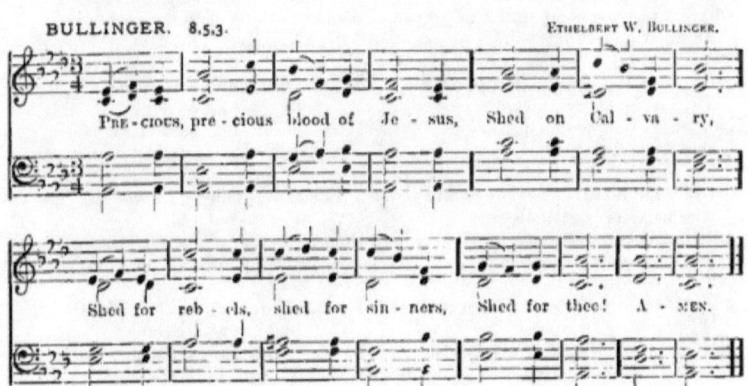

SERENITY. C. M.   WILLIAM V. WALLACE.

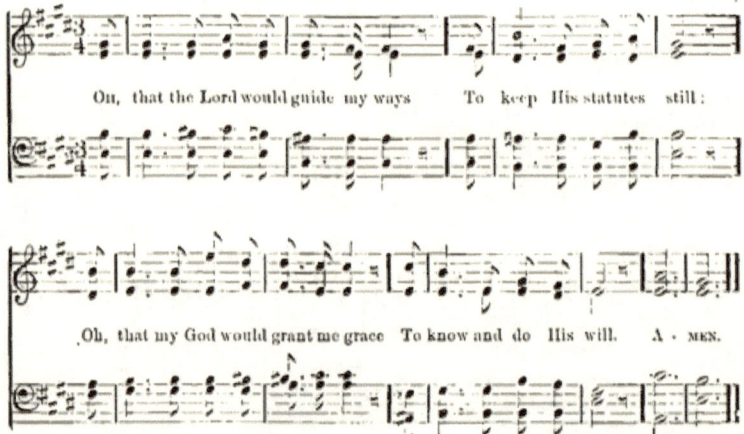

Oh, that the Lord would guide my ways To keep His statutes still:
Oh, that my God would grant me grace To know and do His will. A-MEN.

Used by arr. with O. Ditson Co., owners of copyright.

166

Oh, that the Lord would guide my ways
  To keep His statutes still:
Oh, that my God would grant me grace
  To know and do His will.

2 Oh, send Thy Spirit down, to write
  Thy law upon my heart;
Nor let my tongue indulge deceit,
  Or act the liar's part.

3 Order my footsteps by Thy word,
  And make my heart sincere;
Let sin have no dominion, Lord!
  But keep my conscience clear.

4 Make me to walk in Thy commands—
  'T is a delightful road;
Nor let my head, or heart, or hands,
  Offend against my God.

                    Isaac Watts.

167

Oh, for a closer walk with God,
  A calm and heavenly frame,
A light to shine upon the road
  That leads me to the Lamb!

2 Return, O holy Dove, return,
  Sweet messenger of rest;
I hate the sins that made Thee mourn,
  And drove Thee from my breast.

3 The dearest idol I have known,
  Whate'er that idol be,
Help me to tear it from Thy throne,
  And worship only Thee.

4 So shall my walk be close with God,
  Calm and serene my frame;
So purer light shall mark the road
  That leads me to the Lamb.

                    William Cowper.

Our Faith

168

2 So pure, so soul-restoring,
   Is truth's diviner ray;
A brighter radiance pouring
   Than all the pomp of day:
The wanderer surely guiding,
   It makes the simple wise;
And, evermore abiding,
   Unfailing joy supplies.

3 Thy word is richer treasure
   Than lurks within the mine;
And daintiest fare less pleasure
   Yields than this food divine.
How wise each kind monition!
   Led by Thy counsels, Lord,
How safe the saints' condition,
   How great is their reward!

Josiah Conder.

169

2 The Church from her dear Master
  Received the gift divine,
And still that light she lifteth
  O'er all the earth to shine.
It is the golden casket
  Where gems of truth are stored,
It is the heaven-drawn picture
  Of Christ, the living Word.

3 It floateth like a banner
  Before God's host unfurled;
It shineth like a beacon
  Above the darkling world;
It is the chart and compass
  That o'er life's surging sea,
'Mid mists, and rocks, and quicksands,
  Still guides, O Christ, to Thee.

William W. How.

Our Faith.

GOTT SEI DANK. 7.   Har. by George C. F. Haas.

Spread, O spread, thou might-y Word, Spread the king-dom of the Lord,
Wher-so-e'er His breath has giv'n Life to be-ings meant for heav'n. A-MEN.

170

2 Tell them how the Father's will
Made the world, and keeps it still;
How He sent His Son to save
All who help and comfort crave.

3 Tell them of the Spirit given
Now, to guide us up to heaven,
Strong and holy, just and true,
Working both to will and do.

4 Word of life, most pure and strong,
Lo, for Thee the nations long:
Spread, till from its dreary night
All the world awakes to light.

5 Lord of harvest, let there be
Joy and strength to work for Thee:
Let the nations far and near,
See Thy light, and learn Thy fear.

Jonathan F. Bahnmaier. *Tr.* Catherine Winkworth.

171

Heaven and earth, and sea, and air,
All their Maker's praise declare:
Wake, my soul, awake and sing,
Now thy grateful praises bring.

2 See how He hath everywhere
Made this earth so rich and fair;
Hill and vale and fruitful land,
All things living, show His hand.

3 See the waters ceaseless flow,
Ever circling to and fro:
From the sources to the sea,
Still it rolls in praise to Thee.

4 Lord, great wonders workest Thou!
To Thy sway all creatures bow:
Write Thou deeply in my heart
What I am, and what Thou art!

Joachim Neander. *Tr.* Catherine Winkworth.

130   Our Faith.

WESTON. 8,7. D.   JOHN F. ROE.

Saviour, who Thy flock art feeding, With the shepherd's kindest care,
All the feeble gently leading, While the lambs Thy bosom share;
Now, these little ones receiving, Fold them in Thy gracious arm;
There, we know, Thy word believing, Only there secure from harm. A-MEN.

172

2 Never from Thy pasture roving
   Let them be the lion's prey;
Let Thy tenderness, so loving,
   Keep them all life's dangerous way.
Then, within Thy fold eternal,
   Let them find a resting-place;
Feed in pastures ever vernal,
   Drink the rivers of Thy grace.
                 William A. Muhlenberg.

Our Faith.

ST. RAPHAEL. 8,7,4,7.   Edward J. Hopkins.

Father, Son, and Holy Spirit, I'm baptized in Thy dear Name;
In the seed Thou dost inherit, With the people Thou dost claim,
I am reckoned; And for me the Saviour came. A-MEN.

173

2 Thou receivest me, O Father,
   As a child and heir of Thine:
Jesus, Thou who diedst, yea, rather
   Ever livest, Thou art mine.
      Thou, O Spirit,
   Art my Guide, my light divine.

3 I have pledged, and would not falter,
   Truth, obedience, love to Thee;
I have vows upon Thine altar,
   Ever Thine alone to be;
      And for ever
   Sin and all its lusts to flee.

4 Gracious God, all Thou hast spoken
   In this covenant shall take place;
But if I, alas! have broken

These my vows, hide not Thy face;
   And from falling
O restore me by Thy grace!

5 Lord, to Thee I now surrender
   All I have, and all I am;
Make my heart more true and tender,
   Glorify in me Thy Name.
      Let obedience
   To Thy will be all my aim.

6 Help me in this high endeavor,
   Father, Son, and Holy Ghost!
Bind my heart to Thee for ever,
   Till I join the heavenly host.
      Living, dying,
   Let me make in Thee my boast.

              John Jacob Rambach. *Tr.* Charles W. Schaeffer.

132   Our Faith.

ST. JOHN. C. M.   JAMES TURLE.

Ac-cord-ing to Thy gra-cious word, In meek hu-mil-i-ty,
This will I do, my dy-ing Lord, I will re-mem-ber Thee. A-MEN.

174

2 Thy body, broken for my sake,
  My bread from heaven shall be,
The cup, Thy precious blood, I take,
  And thus remember Thee.

3 Gethsemane, can I forget?
  Or there Thy conflict see,
Thine agony and bloody sweat,
  And not remember Thee?

4 When to the cross I turn mine eyes,
  And rest on Calvary,
O Lamb of God, my Sacrifice,
  I must remember Thee.

5 And when these failing lips grow dumb,
  And mind and memory flee,
When Thou shalt in Thy kingdom come,
  Then, Lord, remember me.
          James Montgomery.

175

O GOD, unseen yet ever near,
  Thy presence may we feel;
And thus inspired with holy fear,
  Before Thine altar kneel.

2 Here may Thy faithful people know
  The blessings of Thy love,
The streams that through the desert flow,
  The manna from above.

3 We come, obedient to Thy word,
  To feast on heavenly food;
Our meat the body of the Lord,
  Our drink His precious Blood.

4 Thus may we all Thy word obey,
  For we, O God, are Thine;
And go rejoicing on our way,
  Renewed with strength divine.
          E. Osler.

Our Faith.

CŒNA DOMINI. 10. ARTHUR S. SULLIVAN.

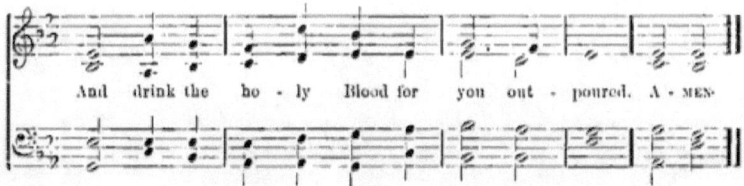

Draw nigh and take the Body of the Lord,
And drink the holy Blood for you outpoured. A-MEN.

176

2 Saved by that Body and that holy blood,
With souls refreshed, we render thanks to God.

3 Salvation's giver, Christ, the only Son,
By His dear cross and blood the victory won.

4 Offered was He for greatest and for least,
Himself the Victim, and Himself the Priest.

5 Victims were offered by the law of old,
That in a type celestial mysteries told.

6 He, Ransomer from death, and Light from shade,
Now gives His holy grace, His saints to aid.

7 Approach ye then with faithful hearts sincere,
And take the safeguard of salvation here.

8 He, that His saints in this world rules and shields,
To all believers life eternal yields;

9 With heavenly bread makes them that hunger whole,
Gives living waters to the thirsting soul.

10 Alpha and Omega, to Whom shall bow
All nations at the doom, is with us now.

Tr. John M. Neale.

Our Faith.

PENITENCE. 6,5. D. — Spencer Lane.

Is the hour of tri-al, Je-sus, plead for me; Lest by base de-ni-al, I de-part from Thee; When Thou see'st me wav-er, With a look re-call, Nor for fear or fa-vor Suf-fer me to fall. A-men.

Used by permission.

177

2 With forbidden pleasures
   Would this vain world charm;
Or its sordid treasures
   Spread to work me harm;
Bring to my remembrance
   Sad Gethsëmane,
Or, in darker semblance,
   Cross-crowned Calvary.

3 Should Thy mercy send me
   Sorrow, toil, and woe;
Or should pain attend me
   On my path below;
Grant that I may never
   Fail Thy hand to see;
Grant that I may ever
   Cast my care on Thee.

4 When my last hour cometh,
   Fraught with strife and pain,
When my dust returneth
   To the dust again;
On Thy truth relying,
   Through that mortal strife,
Jesus, take me, dying,
   To eternal life.

James Montgomery.

Our Faith.

LEICESTER. C. M.   WILLIAM HURST

My God, ac-cept my heart this day. And make it al-ways Thine.

That I from Thee no more may stray, No more from Thee de-cline. A - MEN.

178

2 Before the Cross of Him who died,
   Behold, I prostrate fall;
Let every sin be crucified,
   Let Christ be all in all!

3 Anoint me with Thy heavenly grace,
   Adopt me for Thine own;
That I may see Thy glorious face,
   And worship at Thy throne!

4 May the dear Blood, once shed for me,
   My blest Atonement prove,
That I from first to last may be
   The purchase of Thy Love!

5 Let every thought, and work, and word,
   To Thee be ever given;
Then life shall be Thy service, Lord,
   And death the gate of heaven!
                Matthew Bridges.

179

I AM not worthy, Holy Lord,
   That Thou shouldst come to me;
Speak but the word: one gracious word
   Can set the sinner free.

2 I am not worthy; cold and bare
   The lodging of my soul;
How canst Thou deign to enter there?
   Lord, speak, and make me whole.

3 I am not worthy; yet, my God,
   How can I say Thee nay:
Thee, Who didst give Thy flesh and blood
   My ransom-price to pay?

4 Oh, come! in this sweet morning hour
   Feed me with food divine;
And fill with all Thy love and power
   This worthless heart of mine.
                Henry W. Baker.

Our Faith.

EVERMORE. 7.
HENRY J. GAUNTLETT.

Thine for-ev-er! God of love, Hear us from Thy throne a-bove;

Thine for-ev-er may we be, Here, and in e-ter-ni-ty. A-MEN.

180

2 Thine forever! Oh, how blest
They who find in Thee their rest!
Saviour, Guardian, heavenly Friend,
Oh, defend us to the end!

3 Thine forever! Lord of life,
Shield us through our earthly strife:
Thou the Life, the Truth, the Way,
Guide us to the realms of day.

4 Thine forever! Shepherd, keep
Us, Thy weak and trembling sheep,
Safe alone beneath Thy care,
Let us all Thy goodness share.

5 Thine forever! Thou our Guide,
All our wants by Thee supplied;
All our sins by Thee forgiven.
Lead us, Lord, from earth to heaven.

Mary F. Maude.

181

PARDONED through redeeming grace,
  In Thy blessèd Son revealed,
Worshipping before Thy face,
  Lord, to Thee ourselves we yield.

2 Thou the sacrifice receive,
  Humbly offered through Thy Son;
Quicken us in Him to live;
  Lord, in us Thy will be done.

3 By the hallowed outward sign,
  By the cleansing grace within,
Seal, and make us wholly Thine;
  Wash, and keep us pure from sin.

4 Called to bear the Christian name,
  May our vows and life accord,
And our every deed proclaim
  "Holiness unto the Lord!"

Edward Osler.

Our Faith.

NOTTINGHAM. C. M.   Jeremiah Clarke

Blest be our ev - er - last - ing Lord, Our Fa - ther, God, and King!
Thy sovereign greatness we re - cord, Thy glorious pow'r we sing. A-MEN.

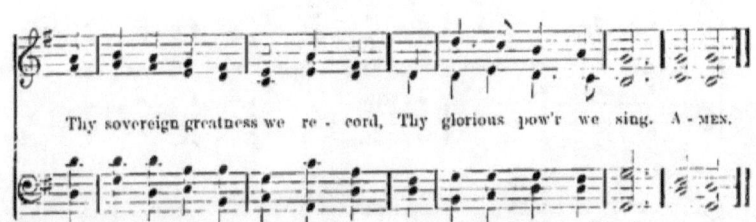

182

2 By Thee the victory is given:
   The majesty divine,
Wisdom and might, and earth and heaven,
   And all therein are Thine.

3 Riches, as seemeth good to Thee,
   Thou dost, and honor give;
And kings their power and dignity
   Out of Thy hand receive.

4 Thou hast on us the grace bestowed,
   Thy greatness to proclaim;
And therefore now we thank our God,
   And praise Thy glorious Name.

5 Thy glorious Name, Thy nature's power,
   Thou hast to man made known;
And all the Deity is ours,
   Through Thy incarnate Son.
                       Charles Wesley.

183

Holy and reverend is the name
   Of our eternal King.
Thrice holy, Lord! the angels cry:
   Thrice holy, let us sing.

2 Holy is He in all His works,
   And saints are His delight;
But sinners and their wicked ways
   Shall perish from His sight.

3 The deepest reverence of the mind
   Pay, O my soul, to God;
Lift with thy hands a holy heart
   To His sublime abode.

4 Thou righteous God! preserve my soul
   From all pollution free:
The pure in heart are Thy delight,
   And they Thy face shall see.
                       John Needham.

Our Faith

JESU, GEH' VORAN. 5,8,5. — ADAM DRESE.

Jesus, still lead on, Till our Rest be won! And although the way be cheerless, We will follow calm and fearless. Guide us by Thy hand To our Fatherland! A-men.

184

Jesus, still lead on,
Till our Rest be won!
And although the way be cheerless,
We will follow, calm and fearless.
Guide us by Thy hand
To our Fatherland!

2 If the way be drear,
If the foe be near,
Let not faithless fears o'ertake us,
Let not faith and hope forsake us;
For through many a foe
To our home we go!

3 When we seek relief
From a long-felt grief;
When temptations come alluring,
Make us patient and enduring:
Show us that bright shore
Where we weep no more!

4 Jesus, still lead on,
Till our Rest be won;
Heavenly Leader, still direct us,
Still support, console, protect us,
Till we safely stand
In our Fatherland!

Nicholas Zinzendorf. Tr. Jane Borthwick.

185

2 Lo, Jehovah, we adore Thee;
　Thee our Saviour! Thee our God!
From His throne His beams of glory
　Shine through all the world abroad.
In His word His light arises,
　Brightest beams of truth and grace;
Bind, oh, bind your sacrifices,
　In His courts your offerings place.

3 Jesus, Thee our Saviour hailing,
　Thee our God in praise we own;
Highest honors, never failing,
　Rise eternal round Thy throne;
Now, ye saints, His power confessing,
　In your grateful strains adore;
For His mercy, never ceasing,
　Flows, and flows for evermore.

William Goode.

140   Our Lord.

AZMON. C. M.   Carl G. Gläser.

Come, let us join our cheer-ful songs With an-gels round the throne;

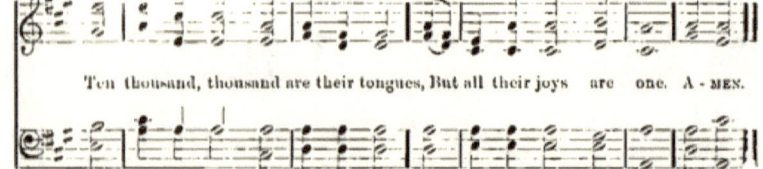

Ten thousand, thousand are their tongues, But all their joys are one. A-MEN.

186

2 "Worthy the Lamb that died," they cry,
  "To be exalted thus!"
"Worthy the Lamb!" our lips reply,
  "For He was slain for us."

3 Jesus is worthy to receive
  Honor and power divine;
And blessings more than we can give,
  Be, Lord, for ever Thine!

4 Let all that dwell above the sky,
  And air, and earth, and seas,
Conspire to lift Thy glories high,
  And speak Thine endless praise.

5 The whole creation join in one
  To bless the sacred name
Of Him who sits upon the throne,
  And to adore the Lamb!
                Isaac Watts.

187

Jesus! I love Thy charming name,
  'T is music to mine ear;
Fain would I sound it out so loud,
  That earth and heaven should hear.

2 Yes! —Thou art precious to my soul,
  My transport and my trust;
Jewels, to Thee, are gaudy toys,
  And gold is sordid dust.

3 All my capacious powers can wish,
  In Thee doth richly meet;
Not to mine eyes is light so dear,
  Nor friendship half so sweet.

4 Thy grace still dwells upon my heart,
  And sheds its fragrance there;—
The noblest balm of all its wounds,
  The cordial of its care.
                Philip Doddridge.

Our Lord.

CORONATION. C. M. Oliver Holden.

All hail the pow'r of Jesus' name! Let angels prostrate fall;

Bring forth the Royal Diadem, And crown Him Lord of all;

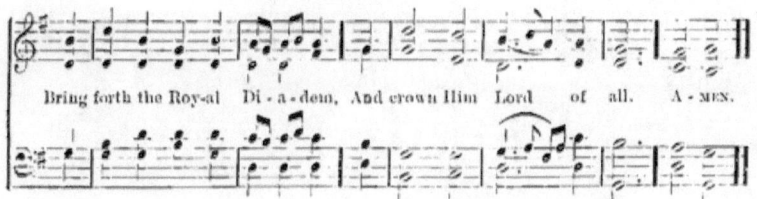

Bring forth the Royal Diadem, And crown Him Lord of all. A-men.

188

2 Crown Him, ye martyrs of our God,
   Who from His altar call;
Extol the stem of Jesse's rod,
   And crown Him Lord of all.

3 Let every kindred, every tribe,
   On this terrestial ball,
To Him all majesty ascribe,
   And crown Him Lord of all.

4 Oh, that with yonder sacred throng,
   We at His feet may fall;
We'll join the everlasting song
   And crown Him Lord of all.
Edward Perronet.

189

Hail, Holy, Holy, Holy Lord!
   Let powers immortal sing;
Adore the co-eternal Word,
   Rejoice, the Lord is King!

2 To Thee all angels cry aloud,
   Thy Name hosannas ring;
Around Thy throne their myriads crowd,
   And shout, the Lord is King!

3 Hail Him, they cry, ye sons of light,
   Of joy th' eternal Spring;
Praise Him who formed you by His might,
   Rejoice, the Lord is King!
Edward Perronet.

Our Lord.

OLIVET. 6,4. LOWELL MASON.

190

Lord of all power and might,
Father of love and light,
　Speed on Thy word:
O let the gospel sound
All the wide world around,
Wherever man is found:
　God speed His word.

2 Hail, blessed Jubilee:
Thine, Lord, the glory be;
　Hallelujah!
Thine was the mighty plan,
From Thee the work began;
Away with praise of man,
　Glory to God!

3 Lo, what embattled foes,
Stern in their hate, oppose
　God's holy word:
One for His truth we stand,
Strong in His own right hand,
Firm as a martyr-band:
　God shield His word.

4 Onward shall be our course,
Despite of fraud or force;
　God is before:
His word ere long shall run
Free as the noon-day sun;
His purpose must be done:
　God bless His word.

Hugh Stowell.

Our Lord.

FEDERAL STREET. L. M.   Henry K. Oliver.

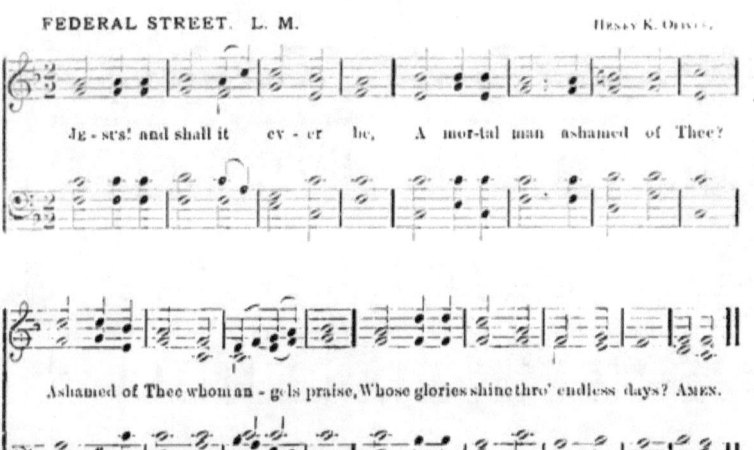

Jesus! and shall it ever be, A mortal man ashamed of Thee? Ashamed of Thee whom an-gels praise, Whose glories shine thro' endless days? Amen.

191

2 Ashamed of Jesus! sooner far
Let evening blush to own a star;
He sheds the beams of light divine
O'er this benighted soul of mine.

3 Ashamed of Jesus! that dear Friend
On whom my hopes of heaven depend!
No; when I blush, be this my shame,
That I no more revere His name.

4 Ashamed of Jesus! yes, I may,
When I've no guilt to wash away;
No tear to wipe, no good to crave,
No fears to quell, no soul to save.

5 Till then—nor is my boasting vain—
Till then, I boast a Saviour slain!
And, oh, may this my glory be
That Christ is not ashamed of me!
Joseph Grigg.

192

Jesus, Thou Joy of loving hearts,
Thou Fount of life! Thou Light of men!
From the best bliss that earth imparts,
We turn unfilled to Thee again.

2 Thy truth unchanged hath ever stood;
Thou savest those that on Thee call;
To them that seek Thee thou art good,
To them that find Thee, All in All.

3 Our restless spirits yearn for Thee,
Where'er our changeful lot is cast;
Glad, when Thy gracious smile we see,
Blest, when our faith can hold Thee fast.

4 O Jesus, ever with us stay;
Make all our moments calm and bright.
Chase the dark night of sin away,
Shed o'er the world Thy holy light!
Ray Palmer.

Our Lord.

RAYNOLDS. 11,10.   FELIX MENDELSSOHN-BARTHOLDY.

We would see Je-sus—for the shad-ows length-en A-cross this lit-tle landscape of our life; We would see Je-sus, our weak faith to strength-en For the last wea-ri-ness—the fi-nal strife. A-MEN.

193

2 We would see Jesus—the great Rock Foundation,
   Whereon our feet were set with sovereign grace;
Not life, nor death, with all their agitation,
   Can thence remove us, if we see His face.

3 We would see Jesus—other lights are paling,
   Which for long years we have rejoiced to see;
The blessings of our pilgrimage are failing,
   We would not mourn them, for we go to Thee.

4 We would see Jesus—this is all we're needing,
   Strength, joy, and willingness come with the sight;
We would see Jesus, dying, risen, pleading,
   Then welcome day, and farewell mortal night!

Anna D. Warner.

194

2 Thine am I by all ties;
   But chiefly Thine,
   That through Thy sacrifice,
      Thou, Lord, art mine.
By Thine own cords of love, so sweetly
      wound
Around me, I to Thee am closely bound.

3 To Thee, Thou bleeding Lamb,
   I all things owe;
   All that I have and am,
      And all I know.
All that I have is now no longer mine,
And I am not mine own; Lord, I am
      Thine.

4 How can I, Lord, withhold
   Life's brightest hour
   From Thee; or gathered gold,
      Or any power?
Why should I keep one precious thing
      from Thee,
When Thou hast given Thine own dear
      self for me?

Charles F. Marks.

Our Lord.

TRIUMPH. 8,7, 6 lines. HENRY J. GAUNTLETT

To the Name of our sal-va-tion Hon-or, wor-ship, thanks, we pay;
Which, for many a gen-er-a-tion, Hid in God's fore-knowledge lay,
But with ho-ly ex-ul-ta-tion We may sing a-loud to-day. A-MEN.

195

2 Jesus is the Name we treasure,
  Name beyond what words can tell;
Name of gladness, Name of pleasure,
  Ear and heart delighting well;
Name of sweetness, passing measure,
  Saving us from sin and hell.

3 'Tis the Name for adoration;
  'Tis the Name of victory;
'Tis the Name for meditation
  In this vale of misery;
'Tis the Name for veneration
  By the citizens on high.

4 Jesus is the Name exalted
  Over every other name;
In this Name, whene'er assaulted,
  We can put our foes to shame;
Strength to them who else had halted,
  Eyes to blind, and feet to lame.

5 Jesus, we Thy Name adoring,
  Long to see Thee as Thou art;
Of Thy clemency imploring
  So to write it in our heart,
That hereafter, upward soaring,
  We with angels may have part.

Tr. John M. Neale.

Our Lord.

196

2 O Bringer of salvation,
  Who wondrously hast wrought,
Thyself the revelation
  Of love beyond our thought;
We worship Thee, we bless Thee,
  To Thee alone we sing;
We praise Thee, and confess Thee,
  Our gracious Lord and King.

3 In Thee all fulness dwelleth,
  All grace and power divine;
The glory that excelleth,
  O Son of God, is Thine;
We worship Thee, we bless Thee,
  To Thee alone we sing;
We praise Thee, and confess Thee,
  Our glorious Lord and King.

Frances R. Havergal.

Our Lord.

CRUSADERS' HYMN. 5.7.8.

Har. by Richard S. Willis.

Beau-ti-ful Sav-iour! King of Cre-a-tion! Son of God and Son of Man! Tru-ly I'd love Thee, Tru-ly I'd serve Thee, Light of my soul, my Joy, my Crown. A-men.

197

2 Fair are the meadows,
  Fairer the woodlands,
Robed in flowers of blooming Spring;
  Jesus is fairer,
  Jesus is purer;
He makes our sorrowing spirit sing.

3 Fair is the sunshine,
  Fairer the moonlight
And the sparkling stars on high;
  Jesus shines brighter,
  Jesus shines purer,
Than all the angels in the sky.

4 Beautiful Saviour!
  Lord of the nations!
Son of God and Son of Man!
  Glory and honor,
  Praise, adoration,
Now and for evermore be Thine!

Tr. Joseph A. Seiss.

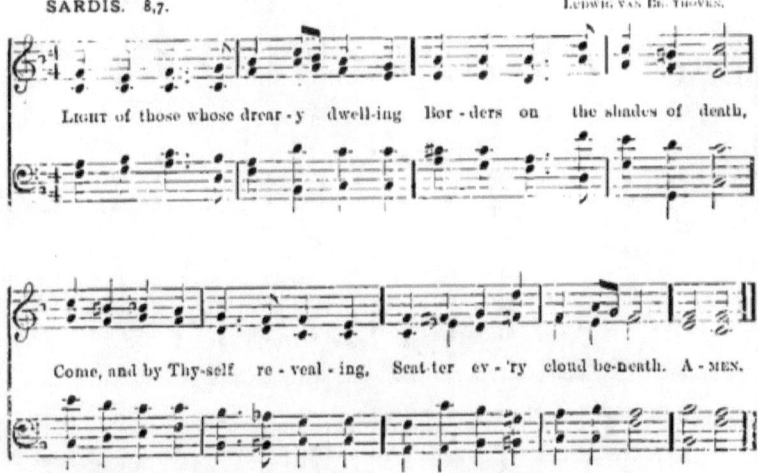

198

2 Still we wait for Thine appearing;
  Life and joy Thy beams impart,
Chasing all our fears, and cheering
  Every poor, benighted heart.

3 Come, and manifest Thy favor
  To our ruined, guilty race;
Come, Thou universal Saviour;
  Come, and bring the gospel grace.

4 Save us in Thy great compassion,
  O Thou mild, pacific Prince;
Give the knowledge of salvation,
  Give the pardon of our sins:

5 By Thine all-atoning merit,
  Every burdened soul release;
Every weary, wandering spirit,
  Guide into Thy perfect peace.
        Charles Wesley.

199

Now I know the great Redeemer,
  Know He lives and spreads His fame;
Lives—and all the heavens adore Him;
  Lives—and earth resounds His name.

2 My Redeemer lives within me,
  Lives—and heavenly life conveys;
Lives—and glory now surrounds me;
  Lives—and I His name shall praise.

3 Pardon, peace, and full salvation
  From my living Saviour flow;
Light, and life, and consolation,—
  All the good I e'er can know.

4 Soon shall I behold my Saviour;
  He who lives and reigns above,
Lives—and I shall live for ever,
  Live and sing redeeming love!
        Richard Burnham.

150 Our Lord.

WINCHESTER. C. M. Thomas Este.

O Jesus! King most wonderful, Thou Conqueror renowned;
Thou Sweetness most ineffable, In whom all joys are found! A-men.

200

2 When once Thou visitest the heart,
    Then truth begins to shine:
Then earthly vanities depart,
    Then kindles love divine.

3 O Jesus, Light of all below!
    Thou Fount of life and fire!
Surpassing all the joys we know,
    All that we can desire,—

4 May every heart confess Thy Name,
    And ever Thee adore;
And, seeking Thee, itself inflame
    To seek Thee more and more.

5 Thee may our tongues for ever bless;
    Thee may we love alone;
And ever in our lives express
    The image of Thine own.
        Bernard of Clairvaux. Tr. Edward Caswall.

201

Jesus! the very thought of Thee
    With sweetness fills the breast;
But sweeter far Thy face to see,
    And in Thy presence rest.

2 Nor voice can sing, nor heart can frame,
    Nor can the memory find
A sweeter sound than Thy blest Name,
    O Saviour of mankind!

3 O Hope of every contrite heart,
    O Joy of all the meek!
To those who fall, how kind Thou art,
    How good to those who seek!

4 Jesus, our only Joy be Thou!
    As Thou our Prize wilt be;
Jesus, be Thou our Glory now,
    And through eternity!
        Bernard of Clairvaux. Tr. Edward Caswall.

Our Lord.

202

Hark, ten thousand harps and voices
  Sound the note of praise above!
Jesus reigns, and heaven rejoices;
  Jesus reigns, the God of love.
See, He sits on yonder throne;
Jesus rules the world alone.

2 Jesus, hail! whose glory brightens
  All above, and makes it fair;
Lord of life, Thy smile enlightens,
  Cheers and charms Thy people here.
When we think of Love like Thine,
Lord, we own it Love divine.

3 King of glory, reign for ever;
  Thine an everlasting crown:
Nothing from Thy Love shall sever
  Those whom Thou hast made Thine own;
Happy objects of Thy grace,
Destined to behold Thy face.

4 Saviour, hasten Thine appearing;
  Bring, O bring the glorious day,
When, the awful summons hearing,
  Heaven and earth shall pass away.
Then, with golden harps, we'll sing,
"Glory, glory to our King."

Thomas Kelly.

Our Lord.

ST. MICHAEL'S. 10,11. GEORGE F. HANDEL.

Ye servants of God, your Master proclaim, And publish abroad His wonderful name; The name all-victorious of Jesus extol; His kingdom is glorious; He rules over all. A-MEN.

203

2 God ruleth on high, Almighty to save;
And still He is nigh—His presence we have;
The great congregation his triumph shall sing,
Ascribing salvation to Jesus our King.

3 Salvation to God, Who sits on the throne,"
Let all cry aloud, and honor the Son;
The praises of Jesus the angels proclaim,
Fall down on their faces, and worship the Lamb.

4 Then let us adore, and give Him His right,
All glory and power, all wisdom and might;
All honor and blessing, with angels above,
And thanks never ceasing, for Infinite Love.

Charles Wesley.

Our Church. 153

AURELIA. 7,6. D. Samuel Wesley.

The Church's one Foun-da-tion Is Je-sus Christ her Lord;
She is His new cre-a-tion By wa-ter and the Word:
From heav'n He came and sought her, To be His ho-ly Bride;
With His own Blood He bought her, And for her life He died. A-MEN.

204
2 Elect from every nation,
  Yet one o'er all the earth,
Her charter of salvation
  One Lord, one Faith, one Birth;
One Holy name she blesses,
  Partakes one Holy Food,
And to one hope she presses,
  With every grace endued.

3 Though with a scornful wonder
  Men see her sore opprest,
By schisms rent asunder,
  By heresies distrest;
Yet saints their watch are keeping,
  Their cry goes up, "How long?"
And soon the night of weeping
  Shall be the morn of song.
            Samuel J. Stone.

Our Church.

205

2 We love our Church, her form of praise,
   In words of living truth;
To stay the soul when billows roll,
   To guide the steps of youth:
Among God's saints of every age,
   His saints of every zone,
With heart and voice, we all rejoice,
   And worship at His Throne.

3 We love our Church, her form of work,
   The fruit of living seeds;
With her as guide, whate'er betide
   We follow where she leads:
In all she asks, in all she aims,
   We'll join with heart and hand;
Till practice pure alone endure
   To earth's remotest strand.

Chorus.

We love our Church, our Mother Church,
   Because we love our Lord—
Her doctrine pure, her precepts sure,
   Because we love His Word:
We pledge our life, our strength, our love,
   Till service end in song above.

John F. Whittaker.

Our Church.

AUSTRIAN HYMN. 8,7. D. — Franz J. Haydn.

Glorious things of thee are spoken, Zion, city of our God;
He, whose word cannot be broken, Form'd thee for His own abode;
On the Rock of Ages founded, What can shake thy sure repose?
With salvation's walls surrounded, Thou mayst smile at all thy foes. A-MEN.

206

2 See, the streams of living waters,
   Springing from eternal love,
Still supply thy sons and daughters,
   And all fear of want remove:
Who can faint while such a river
   Ever flows our thirst to assuage?
Grace, which, like the Lord, the giver,
   Never fails from age to age.

3 Round each habitation hovering,
   See the cloud and fire appear,
For a glory and a covering,
   Showing that the Lord is near!
He who gives us daily manna,
   He who listens when we cry,
Let him hear the loud hosanna
   Rising to His throne on high.

John Newton.

207

Zion stands with hills surrounded;
  Zion kept by power divine;
All her foes shall be confounded,
  Though the world in arms combine.
    Happy Zion,
  What a favored lot is thine!

2 Every human tie may perish;
  Friend to friend unfaithful prove;
Mothers cease their own to cherish;
  Heaven and earth at last remove:
    But no changes
  Can attend Jehovah's love.

3 In the furnace God may prove thee,
  Thence to bring thee forth more bright,
But can never cease to love thee;
  Thou art precious in His sight;
    God is with thee,
  God, thine everlasting Light.

  Thomas Kelly.

Our Church.

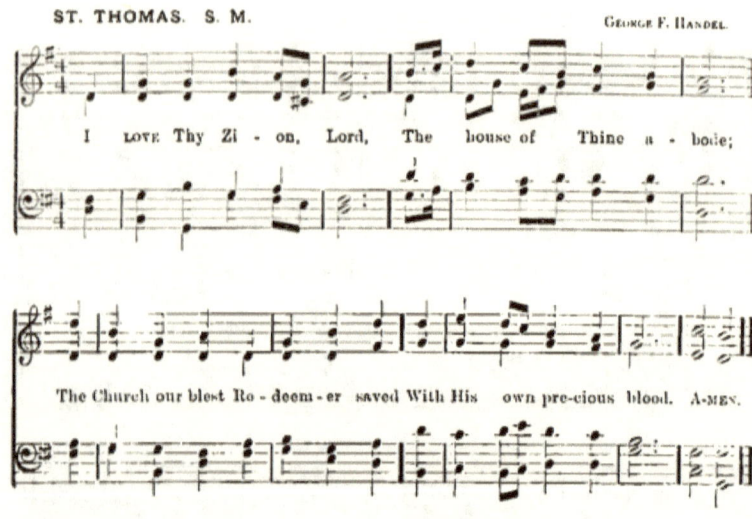

ST. THOMAS. S. M.   GEORGE F. HANDEL.

I love Thy Zi-on, Lord, The house of Thine a-bode;
The Church our blest Re-deem-er saved With His own pre-cious blood. A-MEN.

208

2 I love Thy Church, O God!
  Her walls before Thee stand,
Dear as the apple of Thine eye,
  And graven on Thy hand.

3 For her my tears shall fall;
  For her my prayers ascend:
To her my cares and toils be given,
  Till toils and cares shall end.

4 Beyond my highest joy
  I prize her heavenly ways,
Her sweet communion, solemn vows,
  Her hymns of love and praise.

5 Sure as Thy truth shall last,
  To Zion shall be given
The brightest glories earth can yield,
  And brighter bliss of heaven.
                Timothy Dwight.

209

For all Thy saints, O Lord,
  Who strove in Thee to live,
Who followed Thee, obeyed, adored,
  Our grateful hymn receive.

2 For all Thy saints, O Lord,
  Accept our thankful cry,
Who counted Thee their great reward,
  And strove in Thee to die.

3 They all, in life or death,
  With Thee, their Lord, in view,
Learned from Thy Holy Spirit's breath
  To suffer and to do.

4 For this, Thy Name we bless,
  And humbly pray that we
May follow them in holiness,
  And live and die in Thee:
                Richard Mant.

Our Church.

BOYLSTON. S. M.   Lowell Mason.

Blest be the tie that binds Our hearts in Chris-tian love: The

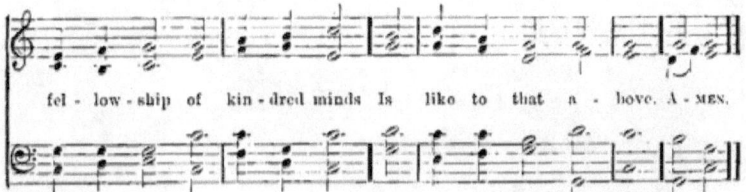

fel-low-ship of kin-dred minds Is like to that a-bove. A-men.

210

2 Before our Father's's throne
  We pour our ardent prayers;
Our fears, our hopes, our aims are one,
  Our comforts and our cares.

3 We share our mutual woes,
  Our mutual burdens bear;
And often for each other flows
  The sympathizing tear.

4 When we asunder part,
  It gives us inward pain;
But we shall still be joined in heart,
  And hope to meet again.

5 This glorious hope revives
  Our courage by the way;
While each in expectation lives,
  And longs to see the day.
                    John Fawcett.

211

Dear Saviour! we are Thine,
  By everlasting bands;
Our hearts, our souls, we would resign
  Entirely to Thy hands.

2 To Thee we still would cleave
  With evergrowing zeal;
If millions tempt us Christ to leave,
  Oh, let them ne'er prevail!

3 Thy Spirit shall unite
  Our souls to Thee, our Head;
Shall form in us Thine image bright,
  And teach Thy paths to tread.

4 Death may our souls divide
  From these abodes of clay;
But love shall keep us near Thy side
  Through all the gloomy way.
                    Philip Doddridge.

Our Church.

CLOISTER. 11,5. JOSEPH BARNBY.

212
Lord of our life, and God of our salvation,
Star of our night, and hope of every nation,
Hear and receive Thy Church's supplication,
  Lord God Almighty!

2 Lord, Thou canst help when earthly armor faileth;
Lord, Thou canst save when deadly sin assaileth;
Lord, o'er Thy Rock nor death nor hell prevaileth;
  Grant us Thy peace, Lord!

3 Peace, in our hearts, our evil thoughts assuaging,
Peace, in Thy Church, where brothers are engaging,
Peace, when the world its busy war is waging;
  Calm Thy foes' raging!
            tr. Philip Pusey.

Our Church.

LEAGUE HYMN. 7,6. D.

To Him who hath commanded That in our youth we give Our hearts unto His service And by His precepts live, To Him our hearts and voices With fervent love we raise, And bring unto His altar A song of pray'r and praise. A-MEN.

213

2 O, Thou who knowest all things,
  The thoughts of every heart,
The motive of each action,
  Each good and evil part;
Look down upon our efforts,
  Though poor and crude they be,
Look down and give Thy blessing,
  For all are done for Thee.

3 And as our League has chosen
  This emblem for its own,
The coat of arms of Luther,
  Thy servant, Lord, alone;

So may we e'er remember
  It's meaning given by him,
Whose memory shall never
  Within our hearts grow dim.

4 And following in his footsteps
  For whom our League is named,
We'll strive unto Thy glory
  O, Lord, to make it famed;
That all may see Thy goodness
  And praises give to Thee,
The Father, Son and Spirit,
  Unto Eternity.

214

2 What though the spicy breezes
　Blow soft o'er Ceylon's isle ;
Though every prospect pleases,
　And only man is vile :
In vain with lavish kindness
　The gifts of God are strown :
The heathen, in his blindness,
　Bows down to wood and stone.

3 Shall we, whose souls are lighted
　With wisdom from on high,
Shall we to men benighted
　The lamp of life deny ?
Salvation, O salvation!
　The joyful sound proclaim,
Till each remotest nation
　Has learned Messiah's Name.

Reginald Heber.

215

2 Hallelujah! hark! the sound,
　From the depths unto the skies,
Wakes above, beneath, around,
　All creation's harmonies;
See Jehovah's banner furled,
　Sheathed His sword; He speaks—'tis done;
And the kingdoms of this world
　Are the kingdoms of His Son.

3 He shall reign from pole to pole
　With illimitable sway;
He shall reign, when like a scroll
　Yonder heavens have passed away:
Then the end:—beneath His rod
　Man's last enemy shall fall:
Hallelujah! Christ in God
　God in Christ, is all in all.

James Montgomery.

216

2 See heathen nations bending
   Before the God we love,
And thousand hearts ascending
   In gratitude above;
While sinners, now confessing,
   The gospel call obey,
And seek the Saviour's blessing –
   A nation in a day.

3 Blest river of salvation!
   Pursue thine onward way;
Flow thou to every nation,
   Nor in thy richness stay:
Stay not till all the lowly
   Triumphant reach their home;
Stay not till all the holy
   Proclaim –" The Lord is come!"

Samuel F. Smith

217

2 Hail to the brightness of Zion's glad morning,
   Long by the prophets of Israel foretold;
Hail to the millions from bondage returning;
   Gentile and Jew the blest vision behold.

3 Lo! in the desert rich flowers are springing,
   Streams ever copious are gliding along;
Loud from the mountain-tops echoes are ringing,
   Wastes rise in verdure, and mingle in song.

4 See, from all lands—from the isles of the ocean,
   Praise to Jehovah ascending on high;
Fallen are the engines of war and commotion,
   Shouts of salvation are rending the sky.

Thomas Hastings.

CAMDEN. L. M. JOHN B. CALKIN.

Fling out the ban-ner! let it float Sky-ward and sea-ward, high and wide;

The sun, that lights its shining folds, The cross, on which the Saviour died. A-MEN.

218

2 Fling out the banner! angels bend
  In anxious silence o'er the sign;
And vainly seek to comprehend
  The wonder of the love divine.

3 Fling out the banner! heathen lands
  Shall see from far the glorious sight,
And nations, crowding to be born,
  Baptize their spirits in its light.

4 Fling out the banner! let it float
  Skyward and seaward, high and wide,
Our glory, only in the cross;
  Our only hope, the Crucified!

5 Fling out the banner! wide and high,
  Seaward and skyward, let it shine:
Nor skill, nor might, nor merit ours;
  We conquer only in that sign.
                    George W. Doane.

219

Jesus shall reign where'er the sun
Does his successive journeys run;
His kingdom stretch from shore to shore
Till moons shall wax and wane no more.

2 For Him shall endless prayer be made,
And endless praises crown His head;
His Name, like sweet perfume, shall rise
With every morning sacrifice.

3 People and realms of every tongue
Dwell on His Love with sweetest song;
And Infant voices shall proclaim
Their early blessings on His Name.

4 Let every creature rise and bring
Peculiar honors to our King;
Angels descend with songs again,
And earth repeat the loud Amen.
                    Isaac Watts.

Our Life.

LUX BENIGNA. 10,4,10.   John B. Dykes.

Lead, kindly Light, amid th'en-circling gloom, Lead Thou me on! The night is dark, and I am far from home, Lead Thou me on! Keep Thou my feet! I do not ask to see...... The dis-tant scene; one step e-nough for me. A-men.

220

2 I was not ever thus, nor prayed that Thou
    Shouldst lead me on;
I loved to choose and see my path; but now
    Lead Thou me on!
I loved the garish day; and spite of fears,
Pride ruled my will: remember not past years.

3 So long Thy power has blest me, sure it still
    Will lead me on
O'er moor and fen, o'er crag and torrent, till
    The night is gone;
And with the morn those angel faces smile,
Which I have loved long since, and lost awhile.

John H. Newman.

Our Life.

LUX VITÆ. 8,7.   Charlotte A. Barnard.

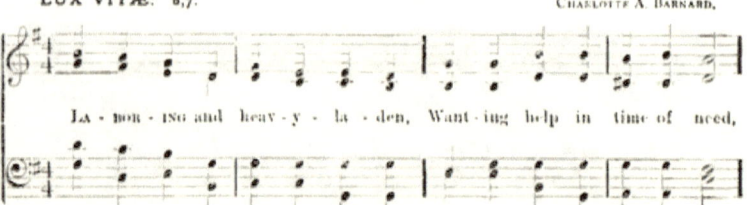

221

Laboring and heavy-laden,
  Wanting help in time of need,
Fainting by the way from hunger,
  "Bread of life!" on Thee we feed.

2 Thirsting for the springs of waters
  That, by love's eternal law,
From the stricken Rock are flowing,
  "Well of life!" from Thee we draw.

3 In the land of cloud and shadow,
  Where no human eye can see,
Light to those who sit in darkness,
  "Light of life!" we walk in Thee.

4 Thou the grace of life supplying,
  Thou the crown of life wilt give;
Dead to sin, and daily dying,
  "Life of life!" in Thee we live.
                     John S. B. Monsell.

222

Jesus, I my cross have taken,
  All to leave, and follow Thee;
Naked, poor, despised, forsaken,
  Thou, from hence, my all shalt be!

2 Perish, every fond ambition,
  All I've sought, or hoped, or known;
Yet how rich is my condition,
  God and heaven are still my own!

3 Let the world despise and leave me,
  They have left my Saviour, too;
Human hearts and looks deceive me—
  Thou art not, like them, untrue;

4 Man may trouble and distress me,
  'T will but drive me to Thy breast;
Life with trials hard may press me;
  Heaven will bring me sweeter rest.
                     Henry F. Lyte.

Our Life.

LABAN. S. M.   Lowell Mason.

My soul, be on thy guard, Ten thou-sand foes a-rise;
And hosts of sin are press-ing hard To draw Thee from the skies. A-MEN.

223

My soul, be on thy guard,
  Ten thousand foes arise;
And hosts of sin are pressing hard
  To draw thee from the skies.

2 Oh, watch, and fight, and pray!
  The battle ne'er give o'er;
Renew it boldly every day,
  And help Divine implore.

3 Ne'er think the victory won,
  Nor lay thine armor down;
Thine arduous work will not be done,
  Till thou obtain thy crown.

4 Fight on, my soul, till death
  Shall bring thee to thy God!
He'll take thee at thy parting breath,
  Up to His blest abode.
                George Heath.

224

A CHARGE to keep I have,
  A God to glorify;
A never-dying soul to save,
  And fit it for the sky.

2 From youth to hoary age,
  My calling to fulfill:
Oh, may it all my powers engage
  To do my Master's will!

3 Arm me with jealous care,
  As in Thy sight to live,
And oh, Thy servant, Lord, prepare
  A strict account to give!

4 Help me to watch and pray,
  And on Thyself rely,
Steadfast to walk on Christ's dear way
  And God to glorify.
                Charles Wesley.

Our Life.

225

2 Like a mighty army,
   Moves the Church of God;
Brothers, we are treading
   Where the saints have trod.
We are not divided,
   All one body we,
One in hope, and doctrine,
   One in charity.

3 Crowns and thrones may perish,
   Kingdoms rise and wane,
But the Church of Jesus
   Constant will remain.

Gates of hell can never
   'Gainst the Church prevail;
We have Christ's own promise,
   And that cannot fail.

4 Onward, then, ye faithful,
   Join our happy throng,
Blend with ours your voices,
   In the triumph-song;
Glory, laud, and honor,
   Unto Christ the King;
This, through countless ages,
   Men and angels sing.

Sabine Baring-Gould.

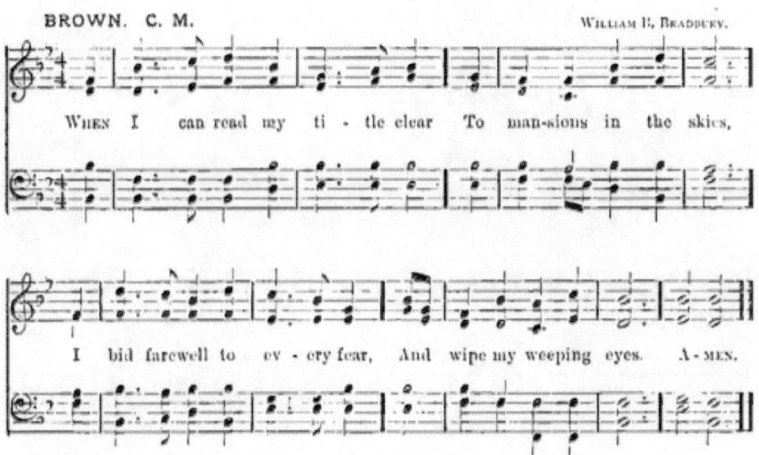

BROWN. C. M.   WILLIAM B. BRADBURY.

When I can read my title clear To mansions in the skies,
I bid farewell to ev-ery fear, And wipe my weeping eyes. A-MEN.

226

2 Should earth against my soul engage,
   And fiery darts be hurled,
Then I can smile at Satan's rage,
   And face a frowning world.

3 Let cares like a wild deluge come,
   And storms of sorrow fall,
May I but safely reach my home,
   My God, my heaven, my all!

4 There shall I bathe my weary soul
   In seas of heavenly rest;
And not a wave of trouble roll
   Across my peaceful breast.

Isaac Watts.

227

2 Work, for the night is coming,
   Work thro' the sunny noon;
Fill brightest hours with labor,
   Rest comes sure and soon,
Give every flying minute,
   Something to keep in store;
Work, for the night is coming,
   When man works no more.

3 Work, for the night is coming,
   Under the sunset skies,
While their bright tints are glowing,
   Work, for daylight flies,
Work till the last beam fadeth,
   Fadeth to shine no more;
Work, while the night is dark'ning,
   When man's work is o'er.

Annie L. Coghill.

Our Life.

HAMBURG. L. M.   Ad. by Lowell Mason.

O Thou that hear'st when sinners cry, Tho' all my crimes before Thee lie,
Behold them not with an-gry look, But blot their mem'ry from Thy book. A-MEN.

228

2 Create my nature pure within,
And form my soul averse to sin:
Let Thy good Spirit ne'er depart,
Nor hide Thy presence from my heart.

3 I cannot live without Thy light,
Cast out and banished from Thy sight:
Thy holy joys, my God, restore,
And guard me that I fall no more.

4 A broken heart, my God, my King,
Is all the sacrifice I bring:
The God of grace will ne'er despise
A broken heart for sacrifice.

5 Oh, may Thy love inspire my tongue!
Salvation shall be all my song:
And all my powers shall join to bless
The Lord, my strength and righteousness.
Isaac Watts.

229

My soul complete in Jesus stands!
It fears no more the law's demands;
The smile of God is sweet within,
Where all before was guilt and sin.

2 My soul at rest in Jesus lives;
Accepts the peace His pardon gives;
Receives the grace His death secured,
And pleads the anguish He endured.

3 My soul its every foe defies,
And cries—'Tis God that justifies!
Who charges God's elect with sin?
Shall Christ, who died their peace to win?

4 A song of praise my soul shall sing,
To our eternal, glorious King!
Shall worship humbly at His feet,
In whom alone it stands complete.
Grace W. Hinsdale.

Our Life.

PASCAL. 8,8,8,6.   Edward J. Hopkins.

O Thou, the con-trite sin-ner's Friend, Who, lov-ing, lov'st them to the end,

On this a-lone my hopes de-pend, That Thou wilt plead for me. A-MEN.

230

2 When, weary in the Christian race,
Far off appears my resting place,
And, fainting, I mistrust Thy grace,
  Then, Saviour, plead for me.

3 When I have erred and gone astray
Afar from Thine and wisdom's way,
And see no glimmering, guiding ray,
  Still, Saviour, plead for me.

4 When Satan, by my sins made bold,
Strives from Thy cross to loose my hold,
Then with Thy pitying arms enfold,
  And plead, oh, plead for me!

5 And when my dying hour draws near,
Darkened with sorrow, pain, and fear,
Then to my fainting sight appear,
  Pleading in heaven for me.
Charlotte Elliott.

231

O HOLY Saviour; Friend unseen,
The faint, the weak on Thee may lean;
Help me throughout life's changing scene,
  By faith to cling to Thee!

2 Oft when I seem to tread alone
Some barren waste with thorns o'ergrown,
A voice of love in gentle tone
  Whispers, "Still cling to Me."

3 Though faith and hope awhile be tried,
I ask not, need not aught beside;
How safe, how calm, how satisfied,
  The soul that clings to Thee!

4 I fear not life's rough storms to brave,
Since Thou art near and strong to save,
Nor shudder e'en at death's dark wave,
  Because I cling to Thee.
Charlotte Elliott.

232

2 Though, like the wanderer,
   (The sun gone down),
 Darkness comes over me,
   My rest a stone,
 Yet in my dreams I'd be
 Nearer, my God, to Thee,
   Nearer to Thee!

3 There let the way appear,
   Steps unto heaven;
 All that Thou sendest me,
   In mercy given;
 Angels to beckon me
 Nearer, my God, to Thee,
   Nearer to Thee!

4 Then, with my waking thoughts
   Bright with Thy praise,
 Out of my stony griefs
   Bethel I'll raise;
 So by my woes to be
 Nearer, my God, to Thee,
   Nearer to Thee!

Sarah F. Adams.

Our Life.

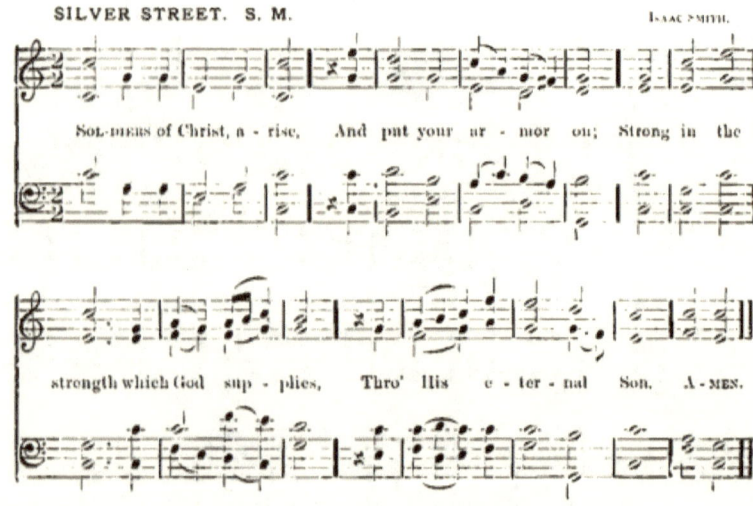

SILVER STREET. S. M.   Isaac Smith.

Soldiers of Christ, arise, And put your armor on; Strong in the strength which God supplies, Thro' His eternal Son. A-men.

233

2 Strong in the Lord of Hosts,
   And in His mighty power;
Who in the strength of Jesus trusts
   Is more than conqueror.

3 Stand then in His great might,
   With all His strength endued;
And take, to arm you for the fight,
   The panoply of God.

4 From strength to strength go on,
   Wrestle, and fight, and pray;
Tread all the powers of darkness down,
   And win the well-fought day.

5 That having all things done,
   And all your conflicts past,
Ye may o'ercome, through Christ alone,
   And stand complete at last.
                              Charles Wesley.

234

Arise, ye saints, arise!
   The Lord our Leader is;
The foe before His banner flies,
   And victory is His.

2 We follow Thee, our Guide,
   Our Saviour, and our King!
We follow Thee, through grace supplied
   From heaven's eternal Spring.

3 We soon shall see the day
   When all our toils shall cease;
When we shall cast our arms away,
   And dwell in endless peace.

4 This hope supports us here;
   It makes our burdens light;
'T will serve our drooping hearts to cheer
   Till faith shall end in sight.
                              Thomas Kelly.

Our Life.

CHRISTMAS. C. M. — George F. Handel.

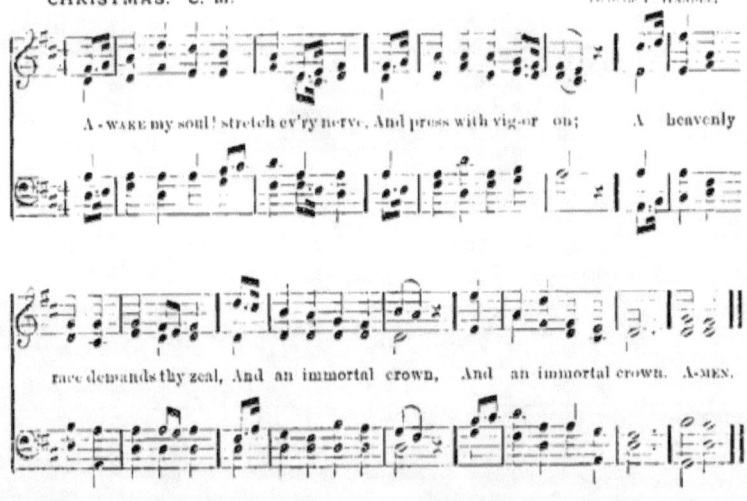

A-wake my soul! stretch ev'ry nerve, And press with vigor on; A heavenly race demands thy zeal, And an immortal crown, And an immortal crown. A-MEN.

235

2 A cloud of witnesses around,
   Hold thee in full survey;
Forget the steps already trod,
   And onward urge thy way.

3 'Tis God's all-animating voice
   That calls thee from on high;
'Tis His own hand presents the prize
   To thine uplifted eye.

4 Blest Saviour! introduced by Thee,
   Have I my race begun;
And, crowned with vict'ry, at Thy feet
   I'll lay my honors down.

5 Then wake, my soul, stretch every nerve,
   And press with vigor on;
A heavenly race demands thy zeal,
   And an immortal crown.
Philip Doddridge.

236

Am I a soldier of the cross,
   A follower of the Lamb,
And shall I fear to own His cause,
   Or blush to speak His name?

2 Must I be carried to the skies
   On flowery beds of ease,
While others fought to win the prize,
   And sailed through bloody seas?

3 Sure I must fight if I would reign;
   Increase my courage, Lord;
I'll bear the cross, endure the pain,
   Supported by Thy word.

4 Thy saints, in all this glorious war,
   Shall conquer, though they die;
They view the triumph from afar,
   By faith they bring it nigh.
Isaac Watts.

237

2 They stand, those halls of Zion,
  All jubilant with song,
And bright with many an angel,
  And all the martyr-throng;
The Prince is ever in them,
  The daylight is serene;
The pastures of the blessèd
  Are decked in glorious sheen.

3 There is the throne of David;
  And there, from care released,
The song of them that triumph,
  The shout of them that feast:
And they who, with their Leader,
  Have conquered in the fight
Forever and forever
  Are clad in robes of white.

Tr. John M. Neale.

Our Hope.

CLARE. 7,6. D.   HUBERT P. MAIN.

In heav'n-ly love a-bid-ing, No change my heart shall fear;
And safe is such con-fid-ing For noth-ing chang-es here.
The storm may roar with-out me, My heart may low be laid,
But God is round a-bout me, And can I be dis-mayed? A-MEN.

Copyright, 1878, by Hubert P. Main.

238

2 Wherever He may guide me,
  No want shall turn me back;
My Shepherd is beside me,
  And nothing can I lack.
His wisdom ever waketh,
  His sight is never dim,
He knows the way He taketh,
  And I will walk with Him.

3 Green pastures are before me,
  Which yet I have not seen;
Bright skies will soon be o'er me,
  Where darkest clouds have been.
My hope I cannot measure,
  My path to life is free,
My Saviour has my treasure,
  And He will walk with me.
                        Anna L. Waring.

180 Our Hope.

JERUSALEM, DU HOCHGEBAUTE. P. M. MELCHIOR FRANCK

Je-ru-sa-lem, thou cit-y fair and high, Would God I were in thee!
My long-ing heart fain, fain to thee would fly! It will not stay with me;
Far o-ver vale and mount-ain, Far o-ver field and plain,
It hastes to seek its Fount-ain And quit this world of pain. A-MEN.

239

2 O Zion, hail! Bright city, now unfold
   The gates of grace to me!
How many a time I longed for thee of old,
   Ere yet I was set free
     From yon dark life of sadness,
      Yon world of shadowy nought,
     And God had given the gladness,
      The heritage I sought.

3 Innumerous choirs before the shining
   Their joyful anthems raise, [throne
Till heaven's glad halls are echoing with
   Of that great hymn of praise, [the tone
     And all its host rejoices,
      And all its blessèd throng
     Unite their myriad voices
      In one eternal song.

John M. Meyfart. Tr. Catherine Winkworth.

Our Hope.

HOMELAND! 7,6,8,6.

The Home-land! Oh! the Home-land! The land of the free-born!
No gloom-y night is known there, But aye the fade-less morn;
I'm sigh-ing for that coun-try, My heart is ach-ing here,
There is no pain in the Home-land, To which I'm draw-ing near. A-MEN.

240

2 My Lord is in the Homeland,
  With angels bright and fair;
No sin is in the Homeland,
  And no temptation there;
The music of the Homeland
  Is ringing in my ears,
And when I think of the Homeland
  My eyes gush out with tears!

3 For loved ones in the Homeland,
  Are calling me away
To rest and peace unending,
  And life beyond decay.
No death is in the Homeland,
  No sorrow is above,
Christ bring us all to the Homeland
  Of His eternal love!

Hugh R. Haweis.

Our Hope.

241

2 Onward we go, for still we hear them singing,
   "Come, weary souls, for Jesus bids you come;"
And through the dark, its echoes sweetly ringing,
   The music of the Gospel leads us home.—*Cho.*

3 Rest comes at length, though life be long and dreary,
   The day must dawn, and darksome night be past;
Faith's journey ends in welcome to the weary,
   And Heaven, the heart's true home, will come at last.—*Cho.*

4 Angels, sing on, your faithful watches keeping,
   Sing us sweet fragments of the songs above;
Till morning's joy shall end the night of weeping,
   And life's long shadows break in cloudless love.—*Cho.*

Frederick W. Faber.

JESUS, MEINE ZUVERSICHT. 7,8,7.   JOHANN CRÜGER.

{ GEN-TLE Shepherd, Thou hast stilled Now Thy lit-tle lamb's long weeping;
{ Ah, how peace-ful, pale, and mild, In its nar-row bed 'tis sleeping!
And no sigh of an-guish sore Heaves that lit-tle bo-som more. A-MEN.

242

2 In this world of care and pain,
   Lord, Thou wouldst no longer leave it;
To the sunny heavenly plain
   Dost Thou now in joy receive it.
Clothed in robes of spotless white,
Now it dwells with Thee in light.

3 Ah, Lord Jesus, grant that we,
   Where it lives, may soon be living,
And the lovely pastures see
   That its heavenly food are giving;
Then the gain of death we'll prove,
Though Thou take what most we love.

William Meinhold. *Tr.* Catherine Winkworth.

Our Hope.

JERUSALEM. C. M.
Alfred S. Baker.

Je-ru-sa-lem, my hap-py home, Name ev-er dear to me;
When shall my la-bors have an end In joy, and peace, and thee? A-MEN.

243

2 There happier bow'rs than Eden's bloom,
 Nor sin nor sorrow know;
Blest seats! thro' rude and stormy scenes
 I onward press to you.

3 Why should I shrink from pain and woe,
 Or feel at death dismay?
I've Canaan's goodly land in view,
 And realms of endless day.

4 Apostles, martyrs, prophets, there
 Around my Saviour stand;
And soon my friends in Christ below
 Will join the glorious band.

5 Jerusalem, my happy home,
 My soul still pants for thee;
Then shall my labors have an end,
 When I thy joys shall see.
Anon.

244

There is a land of pure delight,
 Where saints immortal reign;
Eternal day excludes the night,
 And pleasures banish pain.

2 There everlasting spring abides,
 And never-fading flowers;
Death, like a narrow sea, divides
 This heavenly land from ours.

3 Bright fields beyond the swelling flood
 Stand dressed in living green;
So to the Jews fair Canaan stood,
 While Jordan rolled between.

4 Could we but climb where Moses stood,
 And view the landscape o'er,
Not Jordan's stream, nor death's cold flood,
 Should fright us from the shore.
Isaac Watts.

Our Hope.

REST. L. M.

Asleep in Jesus! bless-ed sleep! From which none ev-er wake to weep;

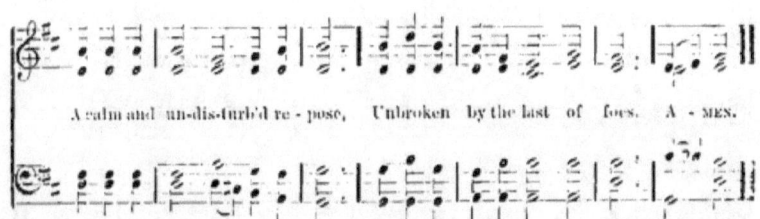
A calm and un-dis-turb'd re-pose, Unbroken by the last of foes. A-MEN.

245

Asleep in Jesus! blessèd sleep!
From which none ever wake to weep;
A calm and undisturbed repose,
Unbroken by the last of foes.

2 Asleep in Jesus! oh, how sweet
To be for such a slumber meet!
With holy confidence to sing
That death hath lost its venomed sting!

3 Asleep in Jesus! peaceful rest!
Whose waking is supremely blest;
No fear—no woe, shall dim the hour
That manifests the Saviour's power.

4 Asleep in Jesus! oh, for me
May such a blissful refuge be;
Securely shall my ashes lie,
And wait the summons from on high.
Margaret Mackay.

246

Why should we start, and fear to die?
What timorous worms we mortals are!
Death is the gate of endless joy,
And yet we dread to enter there.

2 The pains, the groans, the dying strife
Fright our approaching souls away;
We still shrink back again to life,
Fond of our prison and our clay.

3 Oh, if my Lord would come and meet,
My soul should stretch her wings in haste,
Fly fearless through death's iron gate,
Nor feel the terrors as she passed.

4 Jesus can make a dying bed
Feel soft as downy pillows are,
While on His breast I lean my head,
And breathe my life out sweetly there!
Isaac Watts.

Our Hope.

WENN ICH IN TODESNÖTEN BIN. 8,7. Iambic.   Melchior Franck.

1. Great God, what do I see and hear! The end of things created!
The Judge of man I see appear, On clouds of glory seated.
The trumpet sounds; the graves restore The dead which they contain'd before; Prepare, my soul, to meet Him. A-MEN.

247

2. The dead in Christ shall first arise,
   At the last trumpet's sounding,
Caught up to meet Him in the skies,
   With joy their Lord surrounding;
No gloomy fears their souls dismay;
His presence sheds eternal day
   On those prepared to meet Him.

3. But sinners, filled with guilty fears,
   Behold His wrath prevailing;
For they shall rise and find their tears
   And sighs are unavailing;
The day of grace is past and gone;
Trembling they stand before the throne,
   All unprepared to meet Him.

4. O Christ, who diedst and yet dost live,
   To me impart Thy merit;
My pardon seal, my sins forgive,
   And cleanse me by Thy Spirit.
Beneath Thy cross I view the day
When heaven and earth shall pass away,
   And thus prepare to meet Thee.

Partly by William B. Col.

Our Hope.

ES IST GEWISSLICH AN DER ZEIT. 8,7. Iambic.

When all with awe shall stand a-round To hear their doom al-lot-ted,
O may my worth-less name be found In the Lamb's book un-blot-ted!
Grant me a firm, un-shak-en faith; For Thou, my Sav-iour,
by Thy Death, Hast pur-chased my sal-va-tion. A-MEN.

248

2 Before Thou shalt as Judge appear,
   Plead as my Intercessor;
And on that awful day declare
   That I am Thy Confessor.
Then bring me to that blesséd place
Where I may see, with open face,
   The glory of Thy kingdom.

3 O Jesus! shorten the delay,
   And hasten Thy salvation,
That we may see that glorious Day
   Produce a new creation;
Lord Jesus, come, our Judge and King!
Come, change our mournful notes, to sing
   Thy praise in heaven for ever.

Bartholomew Ringwaldt. Tr. John C. Jacobi.

Our Hope.

249

2 Zion hears the watchmen singing,
And all her heart with joy is springing,
  She wakes, she rises from her gloom:
For her Lord comes down all-glorious,
The strong in grace, in truth victorious,
  Her Star is risen, her Light is come!
    Ah come, Thou blessèd Lord,
    O Jesus, Son of God,
      Hallelujah!
We follow till the halls we see
Where Thou hast bid us sup with Thee.

3 Now let all the heavens adore Thee,
And men and angels sing before Thee,
  With harp and cymbal's clearest tone;
Of one pearl each shining portal,
Where we are with the choir immortal,
  Of angels round Thy dazzling throne;
    Nor eye hath seen, nor ear
    Hath yet attained to hear
      What there is ours,
But we rejoice, and sing to Thee
Our hymns of joy eternally.

Philipp Nicolai. Tr. Catherine Winkworth.

GORTON. S. M.   LUDWIG VAN BEETHOVEN.

For-ev-er with the Lord: A-men, so let it be;
Life from the dead is in that word, 'Tis im-mor-tal-i-ty. A-MEN.

250

2 Here in the body pent,
  Absent from Him I roam,
Yet nightly pitch my moving tent
  A day's march nearer home.

3 My Father's house on high,
  Home of my soul, how near
At times, to faith's foreseeing eye,
  Thy golden gates appear.

4 Ah, then my spirit faints
  To reach the land I love,
The bright inheritance of saints,
  Jerusalem above.

5 "Forever with the Lord:"
  Father, if 'tis Thy will,
The promise of that faithful word
  E'en here to me fulfill.

James Montgomery.

Dorologies.

1.   S. M.
TO God, the Father, Son,
  And Spirit, ever blest,
The One in Three, the Three in One,
  Be endless praise addressed.

2.   C. M.
TO Father, Son, and Holy Ghost,
  The God whom we adore,
Be glory, as it was, is now,
  And shall be evermore.

3.   C. M. D.
TO praise the Father, and the Son,
  And Spirit all divine,—
The One in Three, and Three in one,
  Let saints and angels join,
Glory to Thee, Blest Trinity,
  The God whom we adore,
As was, is now, and e'er shall be,
  When time shall be no more.

4.   L. M.
TO Father, Son, and Holy Ghost,
  The God whom earth and heaven adore,
Be glory, as it was of old,
  Is now, and shall be evermore.

5.   L. M.
PRAISE God, from whom all blessings flow!
Praise Him, all creatures here below!
Praise Him above, ye heavenly host!
Praise Father, Son, and Holy Ghost!

6.   6, 6, 4, 6, 6, 4.
TO GOD the Father, Son,
  And Spirit, Three in One,
    All praise be given;
Crown Him in every song,
To Him our hearts belong,
Let all His praise prolong,
    On earth, in heaven.

7.   7s, D.
HOLY Father, Fount of light,
God of wisdom, goodness, might;
Holy Son, who cam'st to dwell,
God with us, Emmanuel;
Holy Spirit, heavenly dove,
God of comfort, peace, and love;
Evermore be Thou adored,
Holy, Holy, Holy Lord.

8.   7s, 6 lines
PRAISE the Name of God most high,
Praise Him, all below the sky,
Praise Him, all ye heavenly host,
Father, Son, and Holy Ghost;
As through countless ages past,
Evermore His praise shall last.

9.
HOLY Father, Holy Son,
Holy Spirit, Three in One!
Glory, as of old, to Thee,
Now, and evermore shall be.

10.   7, 6.
TO God the ever-glorious,
  The Father, and the Son,
And Spirit all victorious,
  Thrice holy Three in One;
The God of our salvation,
  Whom earth and heaven adore,
Praise, glory, adoration,
  Be now and evermore.

11.   8, 7.
PRAISE the Father, earth and heaven,
  Praise the Son, the Spirit praise;
As it was, and is, be given
  Glory through eternal days.

12.   8, 7, D.
PRAISE the God of all creation;
  Praise the Father's boundless love;
Praise the lamb, our expiation
  Priest and King enthroned above;
Praise the fountain of salvation,
  Him by whom our spirits live;
Undivided adoration
  To the One Jehovah give.

13.   8, 7, 8, 7, 4, 7.
GREAT Jehovah! we adore Thee,
  God the Father, God the Son,
God the Spirit, joined in glory
  On the same eternal throne;
    Endless praises
To Jehovah, Three in One.

14.   10s.
AND now to God the Father, God the Son,
And God the Spirit ever Three in One,
Be praise from all on earth and all in heaven,
As was, and is, and ever shall be given.

Index of Meters.

Short Meter.

	PAGE
Boylston	159
Cadwell	49
Dover	95
Gorton	189
Laban	169
Schumann	17
Silver Street	34, 176
St. Thomas	158
Thacher	114

S. M. with Chorus.

Marion	110

S. M. Double.

St. Mark's	99

Common Meter.

Antioch	56
Azmon	140
Belmont	45
Brown	171
Christmas	54, 177
Coronation	141
Cowper	73
Dundee	117
Jerusalem	184
Leicester	135
Manoah	25, 69
Melody	4
Nottingham	137
Serenity	126
St. John	132
St. Stephen's	115
Winchester	150

C. M. Double.

Epes	61
Ellacombe	106
Sears	64
Vox Dilecti	116

Long Meter.

Camden	166
Canonbury	1
Crux Beata	77
Erhalt' uns Herr	107
Federal Street	143
Hamburg	173
Herr Jesu Christ	13

Long Meter (Continued)

	PAGE
Hesperus	121
Hursley	8
Migdol	46
O Jesu Christ	68
Old Hundred	32
Park Street	37
Piericini	22
Rest	185
St. Oswald	90
St. Vincent	6
Stowell	120
Tallis' Canon	10
Vom Himmel Hoch	62

L. M. 6 lines.

Oh, come Emanuel	59
Paine	102

L. M. Double.
(with Hallelujah)

Komm Heil'ger Geist	90

5, 5, 7. 5, 5, 8.

Crusader's Hymn	148

5, 5, 8. 8, 5, 5.

Jesu, Geh' Voran	138

6, 4, 6, 4. 6, 6, 6, 4.

Bethany	175

6, 4, 6, 4, 10, 10.

Budleigh	145

6, 4, 6, 6.

Sunset	11

6, 6, 4. 6, 6, 6, 6.

America	101
Fiat Lux	70
Olivet	75, 142
Italian Hymn	14

6, 5. 8 lines.

Asaph	112
Penitence	134
Praise	30
St. David	113

Index of Meters.

6, 5. 8 lines.
(with Chorus.)
Angels........................ 86
St. Gertrude................. 170

6, 5. 12 lines.
Watchword................... 111

6, 6, 6, 6, 6, 6.
Whittingham................. 119

6, 6, 6, 6, 8, 8.
St. Peter's................... 39

6, 6, 9, 9, 6, 6.
Silent Night.................. 62

6, 7, 6, 7, 6, 6, 6, 6.
Nun danket................... 29

7s, 4 lines.
Cyprus........................ 98
Dijon......................... 26
Evermore..................... 136
Gott sei Dank............. 51, 129
Hendon....................... 15
Horton........................ 23
Montgomery.................. 48
Mercy......................... 92
Rosefield..................... 40
Seymour....................... 5

7s, 4 lines.
(with Hallelujah.)
Ascension.................... 88
Christ ist Erstanden......... 84
Straf mich nicht............. 80

7s, 6 lines.
Dix........................... 67
Muriel........................ 97
Spanish Hymn................ 124
Sabbath....................... 43
St. Christopher.............. 42
Toplady...................... 122
Morgenglanz der.............. 47

7s, Double.
Martyn....................... 118
Mendelssohn.................. 163
St. George's................. 103

7, 6, 7, 5. Double.
Work.......................... 172

7, 6, 7, 5, 7, 6, 7, 6.
(with Chorus.)
Rally Hymn................... 100

7, 6, 7, 6.
Christus der ist mein leben.. 27
Rudolstadt................... 89

7, 6, Double.
Aurelia...................... 153
Bentley...................... 127
Chenies....................... 96
Celeste...................... 128
Clare........................ 179
Day of Rest................... 44
Ewing........................ 178
Herzlich thut mich verlangen. 74
League Hymn.................. 161
Missionary Hymn.............. 162
Norwich...................... 147
Oriens....................... 164
Rotterdam..................... 87
St. Theodulph................. 58
Webb.......................... 53

7s, and 6s, Double.
(with Chorus.)
Dresden...................... 104

7, 6, 7, 6, 7, 6, 8, 6.
Homeland..................... 181

7, 8, 7, 8, 7, 7.
Jesus meine Zuversicht.... 81, 183

7, 8, 7, 8, 8, 8.
Liebster Jesu................. 12

8, 3, 8, 4, 4.
Bethlehem..................... 63

8, 4, 7, 8, 4, 7.
Columbia College.............. 3

8, 5, 8, 3.
Bullinger.................... 125
Erfurth...................... 125

8, 7, 8, 7.
Arundel....................... 21
Devotion...................... 66
Gertrude...................... 65
Lux Vitæ..................... 168
Rathbun....................... 72
Sardis....................... 149

Index of Meters.

8s, 7s, 6 lines.
Triumph.................................146

8s, 7s, Double.
Austrian Hymn..........................156
Autumn................................139
Faben..................................38
Ripley..................................24
Salvator................................9
Sanctuary..............................52
Schouler...............................78
St. Hilary..............................76
Weston................................130

8s, 7s, Double.
(with Chorus.)
Christ is Risen.........................82

8, 7, 8, 7, 4, 7.
Lo! He comes..........................57
Sicilian Hymn..........................18
St. Agatha............................157
St. Raphael...........................131

8, 7, 8, 7, 7, 7.
Gott des Himmels......................2
Ilkley.................................20
Komm, O Komm, du Geist..............93
Krossing..............................151
Unser Herrscher, Unser König...16, 85

8, 7, 8, 7, 7, 7, 7, 7.
Jesu, meines Lebens....................79

8, 7, 8, 7, 7, 7, 8, 8.
Freu' dich sehr........................55

8, 7, 8, 7, 8, 8, 7.
(Iambic)
Allein Gott............................28
Es ist gewisslich.....................187
Wenn ich in Todes nöten..............186

8s, 6s, 8 lines.
(with Chorus.)
Church................................154

8, 8, 8, 6.
Pascal................................174

8, 8, 8, 8, 8, 8, 6, 6.
Macht hoch die........................50

10, 4, 10, 4, 10, 10.
Lux Benigna..........................167

10, 6, 7, 6.
Jerusalem, du Hochgebaute............180

10, 10, 10, 10.
Coena Domini.........................133
Ellers.................................19
Eventide...............................7

10s, 4 lines.
(Peculiar.)
Leila..................................33

10, 10, 11, 11.
Lyons.................................35
St. Michael's.........................152

11, 10, 11, 10.
Alma.................................123
Brightest and Best.....................71
Jeffery's..............................36
Raynolds.............................144
Wesley...............................165

11, 11, 11, 5.
Cloister..............................166

11, 11, 11, 11.
Adeste Fideles........................60

11, 10, 11, 10, 9, 11.
Hark! my Soul.......................182

12, 13, 13, 10.
Nicæa.................................41

14, 14, 4, 7, 8.
Lobe den Herren......................31

P. M.
Ein Feste Burg.......................105
Jerusalem, du Hochgebaute...........180
O Heil'ger Geist......................94
Victory..............................108
Wachet Auf..........................188

Alphabetical Index of Tunes.

A

	PAGE
Adeste Fideles	60
Allein Gott	28
Alma	123
America	101
Angels	86
Antioch	56
Arundel	21
Asaph	112
Ascension	88
Aurelia	153
Austrian Hymn	156
Autumn	139
Azmon	140

B

Belmont	45
Bentley	127
Bethany	175
Bethlehem	63
Boylston	159
Brightest and Best	71
Brown	171
Budleigh	145
Bullinger	125

C

Cadwell	49
Coena Domini	133
Camden	166
Canonbury	1
Celeste	128
Chenies	96
Christ ist Erstanden	84
Christ is Risen	82
Christmas	54, 177
Christus der ist mein leben	27
Church	154
Clare	179
Cloister	160
Columbia College	3
Coronation	141
Cowper	73
Crusader's Hymn	148
Crux Beata	77
Cyprus	98

D

Day of Rest	44
Devotion	66
Dijon	26
Dix	67
Dover	95

D (Continued)

	PAGE
Doxologies	190
Dundee	117
Dresden	104

E

Ein Feste Burg	105
Ellacombe	106
Ellers	19
Epes	61
Erhalt' uns Herr	107
Erfurth	125
Es ist gewisslich	187
Eventide	7
Evermore	136
Ewing	178

F

Faben	38
Federal Street	143
Fint Lux	70
Freu' dich sehr	55

G

Gertrude	65
Gorton	189
Gott des Himmels	2
Gott sei Dank	51, 129

H

Hamburg	173
Hark! my Soul	182
Hendon	15
Herr Jesu Christ	13
Herzlich thut mich verlangen	74
Hesperus	121
Homeland	181
Horton	23
Hursley	8

I

Ilkley	20
Italian Hymn	14

J

Jeffery's	36
Jerusalem	184
Jerusalem, du Hochgebaute	180
Jesu, Geh' Voran	138
Jesu, meines Lebens	79
Jesus meine Zuversicht	81, 183

K

Komm Heil'ger Geist	90
Komm, O Komm, du Geist	93
Krossing	151

Alphabetical Index of Tunes. 195

L

	PAGE
Laban	169
League Hymn	161
Leicester	135
Leila	33
Liebster Jesu	12
Lobe den Herren	31
Lo! He comes	57
Lux Benigna	167
Lux Vitæ	168
Lyons	35

M

Macht hoch die	50
Manoah	25, 69
Marion	110
Martyn	118
Melody	4
Mendelssohn	163
Mercy	92
Migdol	46
Missionary Hymn	162
Montgomery	48
Morgenglanz der	47
Muriel	97

N

Nicæa	41
Norwich	147
Nottingham	137
Nun danket	29

O

O Heil'ger Geist	94
O Jesu Christ	68
Oh, come Emanuel	59
Old Hundred	32
Olivet	75, 142
Oriens	164

P

Paine	102
Park Street	37
Pascal	174
Penitence	134
Piericini	22
Praise	30

R

Rally Hymn	100
Rathbun	72
Raynolds	144
Rest	185
Ripley	24
Rosefield	40
Rotterdam	87
Rudolstadt	89

S

Sabbath	43
Salvator	9

S (Continued)

	PAGE
Sanctuary	52
Sardis	149
Schouler	78
Schumann	17
Sears	64
Serenity	126
Seymour	5
Sicilian Hymn	18
Silent Night	62
Silver Street	34, 176
Spanish Hymn	124
St. Agatha	157
St. Christopher	42
St. David	113
St. George's	103
St. Gertrude	170
St. Hilary	76
St. John	132
St. Mark's	99
St. Michael's	152
St. Oswald	90
St. Peter's	39
St. Raphael	131
St. Stephen's	115
St. Theodulph	58
St. Thomas	158
St. Vincent	6
Stowell	120
Straf mich nicht	80
Sunset	11

T

Tallis' Canon	10
Thacher	114
Toplady	122
Triumph	146

U

Unser Herrscher, Unser Konig	16, 85

V

Victory	108
Vom Himmel Hoch	62
Vox Dilecti	116

W

Wachet Auf	188
Watchword	111
Webb	53
Wenn ich in Todes noten	186
Wesley	165
Weston	130
Whittingham	119
Winchester	150
Work	172

Index of First Lines.

A

	No.
A Babe is born in Bethlehem	87
A charge to keep I have	224
A few more years shall roll	134
A mighty fortress is our God	140
Abide with me, fast falls the	9
Abide with us, our Saviour	40
According to thy gracious Word	174
Again as evening's shadow falls	11
Alas! and did my Saviour bleed	103
All glory be to God on High	42
All hail the power of Jesus' name	188
All people that on earth do dwell	19
All praise to thee, my God, this night	13
All that I was, my sin, my guilt	154
Am I a soldier of the cross	236
Ancient of days, who sittest, throned	52
Another day is past	16
Arise, the Kingdom is at hand	75
Arise, ye saints, arise!	234
Asleep in Jesus, blessed sleep	245
As with gladness men of old	93
At the name of Jesus	148
Awake my soul, and with the sun	1
Awake my soul! stretch every nerve	235
Awhile in spirit, Lord, to thee	108

B

Beautiful Saviour!	197
Before Jehovah's awful throne	46
Blessed Jesus, at thy word	17
Blessed Saviour! thee I love	164
Blessing, and honor, and glory	48
Blest be our everlasting Lord	182
Blest be the tie that binds	210
Blest day of God! most calm	63
Brightest and best of the sons	99
Bright was the guiding star that led	96

C

Christ is risen! Hallelujah!	114
Christ, the Life of all the living	110
Christ the Lord is risen again	111
Christ the Lord is risen to-day	115
Come hither, ye faithful	83
Come, Holy Ghost, our souls	122
Come, Holy Spirit, come	129
Come, Holy Spirit, God and Lord	123
Come, let us join our cheerful songs	186
Come, my soul, thou must be	3

C (Continued)

	NO
Come, my soul, thy suit prepare	33
Come, O come thou quickening	126
Come, sound His praise abroad	49
Come, thou Almighty King	20
Come, thou long expected Jesus	73
Come, ye disconsolate, where'er ye	162
Come, ye thankful people, come	138
Comfort, comfort ye my people	77
Crown His head with endless	185

D

Dear Saviour, we are thine	211
Draw nigh and take the body of	176
Draw us to thee, Lord Jesus	121

E

Earth has many a noble city	91

F

Father, Son, and Holy Spirit	173
Father, who the light this day	60
Fling out the banner! let it float	218
For all thy saints, O Lord	209
For the mercies of the day	7
For thy mercy and thy grace	132
Forever with the Lord	250
Forward! be our watchword	146
From every stormy wind that blows	158
From Greenland's icy mountains	214

G

Gentle Shepherd thou hast stilled	243
Glorious things of thee are spoken	206
God hath sent His angels	117
God moves in a mysterious way	151
God who madest earth and heaven	2
Good news from heaven the angels	85
Gracious Spirit, love divine	125
Great God, to thee my evening song	8
Great God, what do I see and hear!	247

H

Hail, Holy, Holy, Holy Lord!	189
Hail the day that sees Him rise	119
Hail thou once despised Jesus!	106
Hail thou source of every blessing	92
Hail to the brightness of Zion's glad	217
Hail to the Lord's anointed	74
Hark! hark my soul angelic	241
Hark! ten thousand harps and	202

Index of First Lines.   197

H (Continued) NO.

Hark! the song of Jubilee.........215
Hark! what mean those holy voices 89
Heaven and earth and sea and air...171
Heavenly Father, send thy blessing 29
He is risen, He is risen.............116
Holy and reverend is the name....183
Holy Ghost! with light divine.....124
Holy, Holy, Holy Lord!............ 57
Holy, Holy, Holy! Lord God..... 59
Holy Spirit, Lord of light..........131
How pleasant, how divinely fair... 64

I

I am not worthy, Holy Lord.......179
I heard the voice of Jesus say 153
I lift my heart to thee..............194
I love thy Zion, Lord.............208
I thirst, thou wounded lamb of God 160
In heavenly love abiding..........238
In the cross of Christ I glory......100
In the hour of trial................177
It came upon the midnight clear...88

J

Jerusalem my happy home........243
Jerusalem the golden..............237
Jerusalem thou city fair and high ..239
Jesus, and shall it ever be.........191
Jesus Christ is risen to day........112
Jesus Christ, my sure defence....113
Jesus, I love thy charming name...187
Jesus, I my cross have taken......222
Jesus, lover of my soul...........156
Jesus, Master, whose I am........163
Jesus shall reign where'er the sun..219
Jesus, still lead on................184
Jesus, Sun of righteousness 66
Jesus the very thought of thee.....201
Jesus thou joy of loving hearts ...192
Joy to the world, the Lord is come. 78
Just as I am, without one plea.....159

L

Laboring and heavy laden.........221
Lead kindly Light, amid the......220
Let the earth now praise the Lord. 72
Lift your heads ye mighty gates... 71
Light of those whose dreary......198
Lo! He comes with clouds....... 79
Look from thy sphere of endless... 95
Lord dismiss us with thy blessing . 26
Lord God, the Holy Ghost!.......128

L (Continued) NO

Lord! I cannot let thee go........ 34
Lord in the morning thou shalt hear 5
Lord Jesus, by thy passion 41
Lord Jesus Christ be present now . 78
Lord Jesus Christ, with us abide . 143
Lord, keep us steadfast in thy word 142
Lord, not to us, —we claim 141
Lord, now we part in thy blest.... 32
Lord of all power and might......102
Lord of our life and God of our . 212
Lord of the harvest, thee we hail! .137
Lord, teach us how to pray aright . 36
Lord, thy glory fills the heaven.... 55
Lord we come before thee now.... 21
Lord! when we bend before thy... 37
Love Divine, all love excelling.... 35

M

Mortals awake, with angels join... 76
My country, 'tis of thee..........136
My faith looks up to thee.........105
My God, accept my heart this day..178
My soul complete in Jesus stands .229
My soul, be on thy guard.........223
My times are in thy hand.........150

N

Nearer, my God, to thee..........232
Now I know the great Redeemer. 199
Now thank we all our God 43
Now that the sun is beaming...... 4

O

O bless the Lord, my soul......... 50
O Christ, our true and only light.. 94
O Christ, thou hast ascended.....120
O come, loud anthems let us sing.. 53
O day of rest and gladness....... 62
O enter, Lord thy temple......... 130
O God of Jacob, by whose hand ..152
O God unseen, yet ever near.....175
O Holy Saviour! friend unseen....231
O Holy Spirit, enter in...........127
O how shall I receive thee........ 80
O Jesus! king most wonderful....200
O sacred Head, now wounded....104
O Saviour, precious Saviour......196
O thou that hear'st when sinners ..228
O thou the contrite sinner's friend 230
O word of God incarnate......... 169
O worship the King all glorious... 51
O'er mountain tops the mount of God 97
Oh Christians! leagued together. 135
Oh come, oh come, Emmanuel.... 82

Index of First Lines.

O (Continued)

	NO.
Oh for a closer walk with God	167
Oh, that the Lord would guide my	166
Once more before we part	24
Onward, Christian soldiers	225
Open now thy gates of beauty	23

P

Pardoned through redeeming grace	181
Pleasant are thy courts above	68
Praise the Lord of heaven	44
Praise to the Lord! the almighty	45
Precious, precious blood of Jesus	165

R

Rejoice all ye believers	81
Rejoice, ye pure in heart	145
Rock of ages, cleft for me	161

S

Safely through another week	61
Saviour, again, to thy dear name	27
Saviour! all my sins confessing	30
Saviour, blessed saviour	147
Saviour breathe an evening blessing	12
Saviour, now the day is ending	28
Saviour, who thy flock art feeding	172
Shepherds! hail the wondrous	90
Shine on our souls, eternal God	155
Silent night! Holy night!	86
Sing, my soul, His wondrous love	58
Softly now the light of day	6
Soldiers of Christ, arise	233
Spread, O spread, thou mighty	170
Stealing from the world away	38
Stricken, smitten and afflicted	101
Sweet Saviour, bless us ere we go	31
Sweet the moments rich in blessing	109
Sweet the time exceeding sweet	22
Sun of my soul thou Saviour dear	10

T

	NO.
The Church's one foundation	204
The day of resurrection	118
The heavens declare His glory	168
The Homeland! oh, the Homeland	240
The Lord my shepherd is	149
The morning light is breaking	216
The sun is sinking fast	15
The swift declining day	25
There is a fountain filled with blood	102
There is a land of pure delight	244
Thine forever! God of love	180
This day, the light of heavenly	65
This is the day of light	70
Thou whose almighty word	98
Thus far the Lord has led me on	14
Thy life was given for me!	157
To Him who hath commanded	213
To the Name of our salvation	195
To thy pastures fair and large	39
To thy temple I repair	67
Triumphant Zion! lift thy head	54

W

Wake, awake, for night is flying	249
We give immortal praise	56
We love our Church, her form of	205
We march, we march to victory	144
We plough the fields, and scatter	139
We would see Jesus—for the	193
Welcome sweet day of rest	69
When all with awe shall stand	248
When I can read my title clear	226
When I survey the wondrous cross	107
While Shepherds watched their flocks	84
While, with ceaseless course	133
Why should we start and fear to die?	246
With one consent let all the earth	47
Work for the night is coming	227

Y

Ye servants of God, your master	203

Z

Zion stands with hills surrounded	207

www.ingramcontent.com/pod-product-compliance
Lightning Source LLC
Chambersburg PA
CBHW020903230426
43666CB00008B/1294